ALVAR AALTO AND GREECE

TRAILING ARIADNE'S THREAD

Frontcover: *Sketch by Aalto. Delphi from the top of the Theater with the columns of the Temple of Apollo, and in the background, the Tholos, 1953 (© Alvar Aalto Archives, Jyväskylä).*

Backcover: *Two close-up photographs of Alvar Aalto on the deck of* Patris II *during its return trip from Piraeus to Marseilles in August of 1933 (© Hazen Sise fonds, Canadian Centre for Architecture, Gift of the Hazen Sise family).*

Text editing: Freya Evenson
Production coordination: Athina Ragia

ISBN: 978 960 204 406 3

58 Skoufa street, 10680 Athens, Greece
Tel +30 210 3611692, Fax +30 210 3600865
www.melissabooks.com

Printed and bound in Greece

Konstantinos Xanthopoulos

ALVAR AALTO AND GREECE
TRAILING ARIADNE'S THREAD

Introductions by
Juhani Pallasmaa
Dimitris Fatouros

MELISSA Publishing House

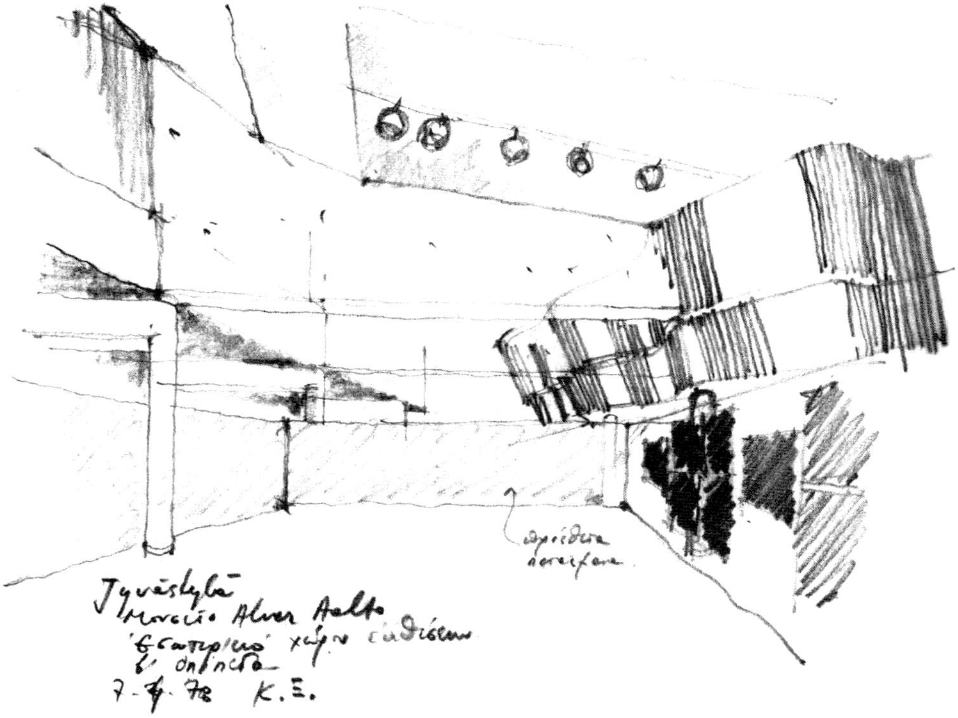

Sketch of the interior of the Alvar Aalto Museum in Jyväskylä, rendered by the author during his "Aalto pilgrimage", April 7, 1978 (© K. Xanthopoulos Archive)

CONTENTS

ALVAR AALTO'S CULTURAL SYNTHESIS
THE ART OF FUSING THE OPPOSITES

Juhani Pallasmaa
Architect, Professor emeritus, Aalto University

> *In every case one must achieve a simultaneous solution of opposites [...] Nearly every design task involves tens, often hundreds, sometimes thousands of different contradictory elements, which are forced into a functional harmony only by man's will. This harmony cannot be achieved by any other means than those of art.* [1]
>
> Alvar Aalto, 1955

During the course of his life Alvar Aalto moved from the restricted world of Finnish country life to ever widening and more refined international settings and personal connections. He fused countless influences and inspirations in his work, and eventually became a significant figure of global architectural and design culture, whose message and lessons are especially pertinent in the confused situation of architecture today. He was born in 1898 in the small village of Kuortane in Southern Ostrobotnia, but moved at the age of five with his family to Jyväskylä, the most important town in Central Finland, where he later attended the Lyceum with a classical curriculum. Due to its landscape setting and cultural ambitions, Jyväskylä was often called "the Athens of Finland".

Already in his youth, Aalto was exceptionally gifted, inquisitive and ambitious. He was a diligent reader, first of books for the youth and later of Western classics. Yet, according to Aalto's biographer Göran Schildt, the two most-read books on Aalto's bookshelves were the anarchist Prince Kropotkin's *Memoirs of a Revolutionist* and the illustrated *Book of Inventions*, an encyclopedia of innovations published in several volumes during the 1930s. These two favourite books reveal the young architect's habit of emulating diverse and even seemingly irreconcilable influences. Throughout his life Aalto rarely mentions thinkers, writers or colleagues of his time. He kept referring to classical sources all the way from Socrates and Dante. Aalto answered Schildt's question concerning colleagues who had influenced his thinking broadly and unspecifically: "I can say generally, that I am a great deal grateful to my colleagues and predecessors, but they are many. It would be a long list all the way from archaic times to our age. It would

1. Alvar Aalto, "Art and Technology", lecture at the Academy of Finland, 1955 in Göran Schildt (ed.) *Alvar Aalto in His Own Words*, Otava Publishing Co, Helsinki, 1997, p. 174.

not only include architects but the entire field of arts and sciences. The list would contain various personalities, and in addition, achievements of architects, painters, sculptors, engineers, and scientists of different disciplines supporting various philosophies."[2]

In his essays, lectures and interviews, Aalto mentions writers like Voltaire, Jean-Jacques Rousseau, Johan Wolfgang von Goethe, Anatole France, Leo Tolstoy, Auguste Strindberg, Henrik Ibsen and Bernard Shaw. Certain philosophers also appear in Aalto's writings, such as Immanuel Kant, Arthur Schopenhauer and Friedrich Nietzsche. With the exception of his short enthusiasm in Functionalist rationality at the turn of the 1920s and 30s, he avoided and criticized orthodoxies, and regarded the architect's work as a task of perpetual innovation rather than the practice of a prescribed discipline and style. In his speech at the 100 Year Celebration of his Lyceum in Jyväskylä he confessed that he supported "a philosophy of doubt". *Ausser sich gehen* [an expression by Goethe], the experience of seeing and judging from other points of view than one's own person and one's own milieu, encourages doubt and scepticism. The much-discussed sceptical world view is in reality a necessary condition for anyone who would like to make a cultural contribution. This is of course dependent on scepticism's transformation into a positive phenomenon, an unwillingness to "move with the stream". On a higher level scepticism is transformed into its apparent opposite, "to love with a critical sensibility".[3]

In his design work Aalto passed through several phases. During the 1920s he produced projects in the prevailing style of Nordic Classicism, inspired by *architettura minore*, the vernacular Classicism of Northern Italy, and he designed furniture inspired by various historical styles.[4] In his short orthodox Functionalist period, Aalto absorbed keenly inspiration from many of the contemporary architects and designers like Le Corbusier, Walter Gropius, André Lurçat, and Moholy-Nagy, who also became his friends. During his early years he was especially inspired by Gunnar Asplund, the Swede in whose office he even sought a trainee job. However, Aalto was usually able to develop ideas introduced by others further than their initiators. He was also active as a writer contributing articles and art criticisms to local newspapers and family journals, sometimes even interviewing himself. He had a keen interest in the visual arts and made pencil sketches, cartoons and carricatures and painted watercolours and oil paintings; in his youth he even considered a career as a painter. These diverse interests were definitely reflected in his professional life in the exceptional range of creative activities

---

2. "Conversation" between Alvar Aalto and Göran Schildt, in Leonardo Mosso (ed.), *Alvar Aalto: Teokset 1918-1967* [Alvar Aalto: Works 1918-1967], Otava Publishing Co, Helsinki 1967.
This formulation of Schildt's question as well as Aalto's response is omitted from the published English translations of the conversation.

3. Alvar Aalto, speech for the Hundred-Year Jubilee of the Jyväskylä Lycée, 1958. Göran Schildt (ed.), *Sketches Alvar Aalto*, The MIT Press, Cambridge, Massachusetts, and London, England, 1985, p. 163.

4. For Alvar Aalto's early furniture designs, see: Igor Herler, "Early Furniture and Interior Designs" in Juhani Pallasmaa (ed.), *Alvar Aalto Furniture*, Museum of Finnish Architecture, Finnish Society of Crafts and Design, Artek, Helsinki 1984, pp. 14-59.

which covered the entire vast scope from regional and urban planning to architecture and product design.

Aalto was simultaneously deeply rooted in Finnish and Nordic cultures, emotionally attached to Mediterranean cultures, and desired to project a cosmopolitan image. He wrote enthusiastically about traditional Finnish farm buildings and the ingenious ways that the only available material, wood, was used by Finnish peasant builders. But he also wrote enthusiastically about the artistic works of Mantegna and Fra Angelico. Regardless of having received a classically oriented architectural training, he turned into a devoted modernist and began to develop a formally and associatively rich, tactile and sensuous architecture of the forest,[5] exemplified by his Finnish World Fair Exhibition in Paris (1936) and New York (1939), and the Villa Mairea (1938-39). "The Northeners, and especially we Finns, are prone to forest dreaming", he once confessed.[6] Sigfried Giedion, the influential Swiss historian, who decisively promoted Aalto's international reputation since the CIAM Conference of 1933 in Athens and on the steamer *Patris II* sailing from Marseilles to Piraeus, emphasized Aalto's Finnish roots: "Finland is always with Alvar Aalto as Spain is with Pablo Picasso and Ireland with James Joyce."[7] On the other hand, Gotthard Johansson, a Swedish architectural critic, observed early on the cosmopolitan orientation in Aalto's persona: "Aalto is a character that one can equally run into in Paris, Berlin, Stockholm, or Turku, a heretic and resourceful thinker who treats architecture as a toy Mecano box. At the same time, he is a refined artist with the same instinctive and assured sense of proportion characteristic of Le Corbusier."[8]

The young Aalto once identified himself with Filippo Brunelleschi and famously desired to turn his modest home town in Central Finland into "The Florence of the North".[9] The fact that Aalto's home town was associated with both Athens and Florence indicates the affective interest of cultured Finns, and specifically of Alvar Aalto, in Mediterranean cultures. In his architectural designs throughout his life Aalto used motifs that refer to Greek culture, such as the amphitheater as a deliberate symbol of culture, democracy and social gathering [eg. the main building of the Helsinki University of Technology (1949/1953-66), currently Aalto University; the North Jutland Art Museum

5. See Juhani Pallasmaa, "Alvar Aalto's Forest Architecture: landscape, geometry and metaphor", lecture at the University of Venice, 21 December 2001. Unpublished revised manuscript, 2004. Juhani Pallasmaa Architects, Archive.

6. Alvar Aalto in Göran Schildt, op. cit., "Architecture in the Landscape of Central Finland", p. 21.

7. Sigfried Giedion, *Space, Time and Architecture: The Growth of a New Tradition*, ninth printing and English edition, Harvard University Press, Cambridge, Mass., 1952. COMPLETE Picasso and Joyce.

8. As quoted in Kirmo Mikkola, *Aalto*, Gummerus, Jyväskylä. 1985, p. 10, trans. Juhani Pallasmaa.

9. See Göran Schildt, "Alvar Aalto-The Early Years", Rizzoli, 1984. In this first biographical volume, Schild writes accordingly: "The ambition [AA's Nordic Renaissance] became particularly real for him when he moved to Jyväskylä, facetiously known as '*the Athens of Finland*'. After his trip to Italy in 1924, Aalto would have liked to see it as '*the Florence of Finland*', and he entered heart and soul into the task of giving Jyväskylä an Italian touch," p. 252.

in Aalborg, Denmark (1958/1966-72) and the Bagdad Art Museum, Iraq (1959) which includes a rooftop amphitheater]. He also used this motif in the courtyard of his own Studio in Helsinki (1952-53), and the Alvar Aalto Medal, cast in bronze, which he designed in 1966 for the prestigious international prize carrying his name. His theater, concert spaces and auditoria also frequently echo the Greek amphitheater archetype. He proposed an open colonnade in the competition project for the Malmi Church of 1951; on the top of a hill the 11 by 4 column grid created an explicit image of a Greek temple ruin. In his project for the courtyard of the Department of Architecture at the Helsinki University of Technology, he had placed eight Greek columns in two rows, obviously intended to evoke the deep cultural heritage and responsibility of architecture.

Also in the grave monuments which he designed Aalto makes references to Greek culture. The grave of Usko Nyström, Aalto's professor in architectural history, is based on an acanthus leaf (1930), which Aalto later used in his design for the graphic emblem of the Finnish Architects Association. The grave of architect Ahto Virtanen, Aalto's relative, who died at a young age, is based on a negative profile of a Hellenic lekythos (1935). Architect Uno Ullberg's gravestone has the motif of an Ionic column volute. Even Aalto's own grave in Helsinki, designed by his widow Elissa, includes an actual Ionic-Composite capital.

The vertical cladding of concrete pilars in strips of stone or wood in his numerous projects emphasize verticality and echo the fluting of classical columns. Aalto even regarded the chair leg as "the little sister of the architectural column",[10] and especially his fan-shaped laminated chair leg reflects the flowing visual character of classical column capitals.

Alvar Aalto's frequent travels in Italy, as well as his architectural and artistic interests and personal friendships are fairly well recorded. Although Greek culture and its early democracy had an archetypal meaning for educated Finns all the way until the emergence of consumerist globalism, and certainly for Aalto, the research of Konstantinos Xanthopoulos is the first thorough study that valorizes the objectives and destinations of Alvar Aalto's two trips to Greece. In addition to his personal visits, Aalto had another source for information on Greek culture. His biographer, intimate friend and interlocutor, Göran Schildt, art historian and writer, lived since the war alternatingly on the island of Leros and the coastal town of Tammisaari in Finland (since 1970 in a house designed for him and his wife by Aalto). Schildt had a passion for Greek culture, sailing in the Greek archipelago and wider Mediterranean, and he must have brought aspects of Greek history, architecture and arts -mythical, ancient and contemporary- to Aalto's attention. In 1957 the two friends sailed together up the Nile River to Luxor on Schildt's boat *Daphne*. Aalto's numerous pencil sketches testify to his interests during his many travels.

10. Alvar Aalto, "The 'Constructive Form'-Exhibition in Stockholm [1954]", in Göran Schildt (ed.), *Aalto In His Own Words*, op. cit., p. 258.

Aalto also included vernacular influences in his unorthodox formal language. Early on he wrote enthusiastically of the wood construction traditions in Karelia and included references to Finnish farm buildings even in his masterpiece Villa Mairea, the family house of a wealthy industrialist and art collector. The tactile qualities of various rattan and wood bindings, especially present in the Finnish World Fair pavilions in Paris and New York and the Villa Mairea, initially derive from an exhibition of Oceanic cultures at the Brussels Exhibition in 1935, which Alvar had visited with his first wife Aino. The refined references to traditional Japanese architecture in the Villa Mairea were inspired by books in his library and most importantly by the *Zui-Ki-Tei* tea pavillion built in 1935 in the garden of the Ethnographic Museum in Stockholm, which became a first-hand source for many leading Nordic architects.[11] Even in his later years, Aalto absorbed influences from his travels. His sketches in Morocco in 1954 are reflected in the solemn ambience of his project for the Lyngby Crematorium in Denmark, whereas the roof shapes and tiled roof edges of his Summer House at Muuratsalo seem to have been inspired by his sketches of Spanish farm houses a year earlier. Alvar Aalto's fusion of modernity and vernacular references brings to mind the significant works of Dimitris Pikionis.

Alvar Aalto's main contribution to modern architecture is the opening up of its strict formal language to include references to other historical phases and cultures, as well as other art forms, especially painting. In the project description of the Villa Mairea he confesses: "The goal was to avoid artificial architectural rhythm in the building without giving up pure 'form', as long as it could be obtained in harmony with the structure or with an increased use of materials and surface treatments that are inherently pleasing to the senses. In this building the designer sought to apply a special concept of form connected to modern painting. He believed that modern painting gives a building and a home a deeper and ultimately more human material and formal accent than an ornament designed as an architectural appendage can."[12]

Having been a devout and vocal Rationalist for a few years at the turn of the 1920s and 30s, Aalto began to criticize the narrowness of the Functionalist and Rationalist positions, and began to promote an "extended rationalism"[13] in his lectures, writings as well as in his own designs. In the new chapter on Alvar Aalto, Sigfried Giedion suggested that Aalto represented "irrationality" in turning standardization into a positive

---

11. For the Japanese influences on Aalto, see in Juhani Pallasmaa, "Image and Meaning", *Villa Mairea 1938-39*, Alvar Aalto Foundation and Mairea Foundation, Helsinki, 1998, pp. 98-100.

12. Aino and Alvar Aalto, "Mairea", in op. cit., p. 31.

13. Alvar Aalto, "Rationalism and Man (1935)", in Göran Schildt (ed.), *Aalto In His Own Words*, op. cit., p. 92.

humane approach.[14] However, Aalto never promoted irrationality, as his deliberate aim was "to expand the rational design method even to the psychological field".[15] Along with Richard Neutra, Aalto was also one of the first architects to see the fundamental biological ground of architecture: "I would like to add my personal, emotional view, that architecture and its details are in some way all part of biology."[16] The biological, evolutionary and neurological perspective in architecture is currently gaining increasing importance.

Subliminal and unspecified references to other historical eras, cultural conditions and the course and effects of time, are a significant part of Aalto's experiential and existential meanings. The Pensions Institute in Helsinki (1949/1952-57) exemplifies how architecture can bring human dignity and a sense of respect to ordinary office work; both employees and clients are received with images of quality and empathy. Some of the spaces, materials and details can even make the visitor to think of the geometric and material splendor of Islamic architecture. The Administrative and Cultural Center of Seinäjoki with its six Aalto buildings (1960-68) suggests an aesthetically refined culture, far beyond ordinary settings. As modernism in general has projected a flat time, a sense of nowness, Aalto's works reflect a deep time, duration and cultural continuity. His materials and details age in a positive manner and turn age, wear and weathering into positive experiences of time. The various buildings of the Seinäjoki Center are deliberately conceived in differing architectural idioms suggesting thus a conglomerate of styles executed by different architects of different eras, although built in fact within a decade. In the Jyväskylä University the main building with its expansive and massive brick walls suggests a medieval defensive structure, whereas the professors' lunch pavilion has the abstracted visual suggestion of a small Greek temple facade creating a striking contrast to the brick buildings around with its white marble accents. This image also reflects the idea of Jyväskylä as the "Athens of Finland".

No doubt, Aalto's visits to architectural sites in Greece, Italy, Morocco, Spain, Egypt and other locations had sensitized him for features and traces of cultural time. Also a lived sense of place, atmosphere and community were essential for him. He intentionally wished to acknowledge "the little man",[17] the unknown occupant and user of architectural settings, in his designs.

14. In 1949 in the eighth printing of the second, enlarged edition of *Space, Time and Architecture* Sigfried Giedion added a chapter on Aalto entitled "Alvar Aalto: Elemental and Contemporary". He introduced Aalto with the following sentence: "Aalto is the strongest exponent of the combination of standardization with irrationality, so that standardization becomes no longer the master but the servant." Sigfried Giedion, op. cit., p. 453.

15. Aalto refers to the impact of psychology in his article "Rationalism and Man (1935)", op. cit., p. 91-93.

16. Alvar Aalto, "Trout and the Stream (1948)", in Göran Schildt (ed.), op. cit., p. 108.

17. Alvar Aalto, "What is Culture (1958)", in Göran Schildt (ed.), op. cit., p. 16.

In 1967 Aalto wrote a short essay for an issue of *Arkkitehti Journal* focusing on the theme of "National-International". The two notions are usually regarded as opposites, but Aalto sees a positive dialogical relation between them: "Seemingly the notions of national and international are regarded as opposites, but it is less likely that in a larger perspective that would be the case [...] perhaps, Erechtheion was originally national, but it became international. This is the case in all art: the final result is always on a wider field than the original source, but this does not exclude that the original source and the final outcome somehow exist next to each other [...] [It is] necessary in a contemporary world, in which the concepts of national and international can hardly be separated from each other."[18]

In his own architectural and design work Alvar Aalto created a unique synthesis taking influences from different cultures and fusing anonymous traditions and modernity, technology and biology, reason and emotion, intelligence and intuition, architecture and art.

18. Alvar Aalto, "National-International" in Göran Schildt (ed.), op. cit., p. 218.

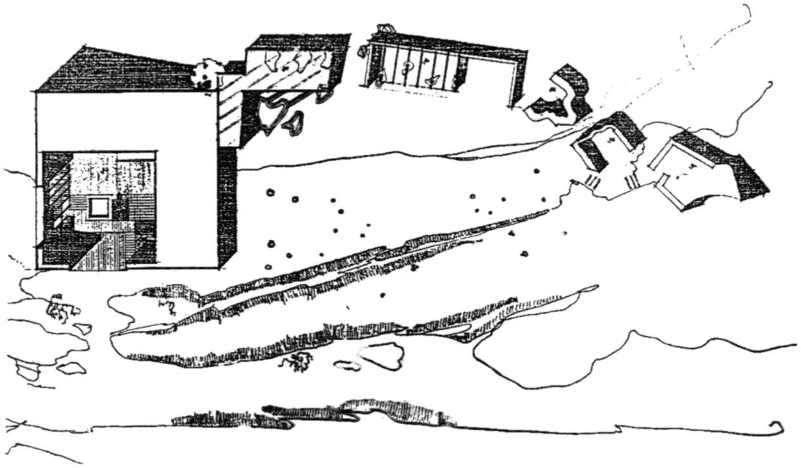

General plan of Aalto's summer (experimental) house on Muuratsalo island. This initial sketch by Aalto shows the main building on the left, connected to a guest wing, and next to them the freestanding woodshed and three unbuilt pavilions, with the architect's painting studio on the far right; all composing an integral and harmonious complex along with the surrounding nature and its physiognomy.

AALTO: THE CEASELESS TRANSITION

Dimitris A. Fatouros
Architect, Professor emeritus,
Aristotle University of Thessaloniki

The architectural work is the trace of habitation; transitions and encounters, possibilities, intentions and rejections, concealment, estrangement and replication.

The multitudes and loneliness, the intensity and the uncertainty of transition and gathering meet the universe of the human body and liberate meaning.

The words persistently seek out definitions and formulations on how to relate the world of the work of architecture to the world of daily life, the pursuits and references to the world of nature, and the co-references and allusions in the encounter with the other and the self.

By removing generalized and simplified expressions, the architecture of Aalto insists on the referential continuity with the profusion of transition and encounter, the multi-faceted nature, the desires, the uncertainties and the arbitrary resorts of habitation, the multi-perceptual sensuality and consistency of everyday life. Insisting on the heterogeneity of touch, Juhani Pallasmaa highlights the dynamics of the world, of the universe of perception.

Classifications and terminologies can easily move the work of architecture away from the dynamic field of the multifaceted identity of reality. Even established generalized associations such as vernacular, classicism, modernism, etc., can limit the field of parallel references, of the unspecified but realized encounter of materiality with void. It is this creative momentum that is confirmed by Aalto.

The world of Aalto's architecture is a ceaseless transition, a ceaseless search for its identity, its indirect and spontaneous multiplicity.

The density of decisions to shape the material condition in its encounter with the density of the natural geographic world confirms Aalto's insistence on the affinity of the materiality of his work with the folds of the soil and the undefined ribs of the articulations of time.

A special way of recognizing and approaching the multitude of Aalto's quests is reflected in his sketches from his trips to Greece.

In the sketches of the "topos" of the theater in Delphi, the insistence on the circular horizontal geometry of the orchestra, on the intensity of the encounter with the variables of habitation, the folds of the earth, the soil and the ruins, the vertical materialities, symbolic references of the habitation's identity become clearly explicit.

The transcultural symbolic dynamics of vertical materiality in the hypaethral world are reminiscent of the outlying linear poles meant for ebb and tide situations in the North Sea, the English Channel and elsewhere.

The notes, sketches from Delphi and Olympia, fragments scattered on the ground of symbolic materialities, columns, tiers and micro-shades of reliefs, the past meets the present as a diachronic, a timeless symbolic potentiality and seeks the words of its multisensory identity. Reiterations are not repetitions.

The experimental, as it has been labelled, house of Aalto in Muuratsalo is an impressive proposition to the array of the trace of the habitation's surroundings, to its encounter with water, the large lake, as well as to the multiplicities of the encounter and the projections of synchronicity.

The main dwelling with the patio, the delimited open courtyard, the basic composite cell, cohabit with three separate small cells and two complex variants, which through their masterful articulation suggest the trail of the borderline in the encounter with the lakeside area. The project proposes a complex multiplicity of the locus of habitation, enclosed, open, with different materialities and geometric identities, a complex conceptual construct of aggregation, as is generally discussed by D. Philippidis, who brings back timeless references to the habitation cell and the development of a place, "topos" of gathering as a concurrent primal stream.

In the totality of dwelling, in this work by Aalto, the references to meeting at the very small scale, the minimum shelter, the isolation of self and the other, converse indirectly or directly with the dynamics of meeting at the large scale.

Even the small scale projects the potential of a truth also pertinent to the very large scale. The conceptual identity seeks its multiple formulations even in the chaotic big city with different genres of materiality and void.

The experimental residence of Aalto in Muuratsalo intersects with the very raison d'être of architecture's creative work, the references of multiplicity, the polysemy, the projection of the disparate and the non-present. With different formulations the infinity of the work's identity constantly seeks the references, the correlations, the disproofs and the verifications. The work of the polysemic world refutes and verifies, modifies and attempts to clarify its active presence even in its everyday applications.

Aalto's quests are a world of multiplicity and sensory tension, a feat of liberating from rankings and classifications, of the recognition that particular entities such as the multi-sensory realities and relative attributions of materiality and void enhance particular creative possibilities.

CONFESSIONS OF A NOVICE
IN LIEU OF PREFACE

A year or so ago, I was asked by Professor emeritus Tom Simons if I would be interested and willing to write a brief account of the interconnections between Alvar Aalto and Greece, and how they could reveal one more significant cultural affinity, amongst the many others which the Finnish architect had lived through and interpreted during his trips south- and westward.

It became immediately obvious to me that I was both interested and willing. But most crucially, was I ready to undertake a task, which both time and space, as well as Aalto's historiography, were not as yet clearly demarcated by any conclusive factual and conceptual boundaries?

As I was pondering, it seemed as if I was only holding the edge of a convoluted thread which I was asked to untangle -something close to Ariadne's thread in front of a labyrinth, whose end and exit lay in darkness, at best, in the shadows of many unknown corners.

Thus, I must confess that I felt literally close to Aalto's "little man" having to confront an unsurmountable challenge; one posed by realities and myths, facts and fiction, inherent on a grander scale in both parts of the Aalto-Greece enigmatic equation.

How should I strive to respond to the challenge? Should I be the architect, the writer, the researcher, or just somebody possessing the eye and the senses, the controlled imagination and the mind, to formulate a plausible thesis?

In this respect, I needed to re-assess meanings of, say, "adequacy", "scholarship", etc. Was I then adequately capable and did I have the knowledge to elaborate and deliver such a thesis, at least in the form of a more or less extensive essay?

Without any sense of pretension, paranoia or short-sightedness, I decided to attribute a relative value to both qualifications, usually appearing as dilemmas in view of any similar demanding and unfathomed challenge. In any case, my humble conviction has been that there could be no limits to adequate learning, information gathering, and critical interpretation, provided that the presence and use of learned common-sense and reason were properties evolving through one's intellect and overall experience. Besides, the idea of an absolute "scholarship" on a matter pertaining to either a particular subject or individual, especially one gifted with such creative capacity as Aalto's, was/is in my view lying beyond any a priori and uncontested adoption and recognition.

This is far from professing that I am lacking genuine respect and admiration for outstanding thinkers, writers and architects who have so far provided excellent historical and critical accounts on the life and works of the great Finnish architect. Reference to such strong minds is anyway unreservedly exposed in my essay, pointing quite to the opposite.

Thinking along these lines gave me therefore the impetus to dare and accept the aforementioned challenge. From the beginning, I confronted it with caution and humility. But, in addition to the logical parameters there was also one which acted as an important motivation. It had to do with sentiments and feelings about Alvar Aalto and about Finland.

While I have been learning to appreciate Aalto's genius ever since my student years at the Polytechnic University of Athens, and later, nourishing further my knowledge and esteem, when experiencing in vivo his major works during a month's trip from Turku to Rovaniemi, back in 1978, a mysterious drive was also pulling me from the Mediterranean Greece towards the north of Europe, most particularly to Finland, as of the mid-1960s onwards. This had a decisive effect on my intellectual and emotional life, and provided further personal assurance to undertaking the essay on Aalto and Greece, with the mediation of Finland and its diachronic culture in architecture.

I therefore saw the challenge not only as any other task in writing about a subject, but also, as a kind of aspired duty, a tribute, which could unveil qualities and propensities, associations and analogies, linking Aalto and Finnish culture to my own country's, and vice-versa.

To this end, the introductory texts written by Finnish Professor emeritus Juhani Pallasmaa, and Greek Professor emeritus Dimitris Fatouros, represent most substantial and symbolic contributions. I feel very thankful and honoured for their assistance, for their confidence and for their presence herewith.

After the painstaking pleasure of articulating and putting together the puzzle of facts and ideas, real and conceivable fictive interpretations, I have finally reached some end; in fact, an open-ended "end", which is hopefully permeable enough to allow and absorb new facts, feedback criticism and thoughts for many amongst those pursuing research and study of Aalto's presence and everlasting contribution to man's intuition, creativity: in short, to architecture.

Konstantinos Xanthopoulos
Helsinki, June 23-25, 2019

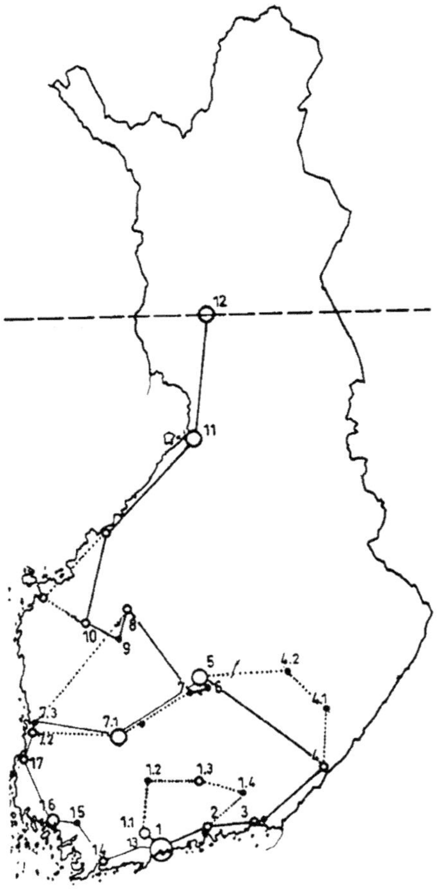

An architectural pilgrimage to Alvar Aalto's works in Finland and Aalborg/Denmark undertaken by the author in March and April 1978 (note: this itinerary was published in the Bulletin of the Association of Greek Architects/Δελτίο Συλλόγου Αρχιτεκτόνων*, 1st issue, Period B, December 1991, p. 51).*

PROLEGOMENA
RE-DISCOVERING GREECE

> *The architect must be a modern person. We cannot build 'in Greek' any more than we can speak Greek to each other.*
>
> Gustaf Nyström[1]

Yet, in the wake of the twentieth century, a "legendary teacher of architecture" such as "late-historicist" Gustaf Nyström (1856-1917), was setting his own imprint on the heritage of Classical and Hellenistic Greece, and its metaphorical significance both in the education and practice of architecture in Finland. In spite of his ambiguous quotation on *modern* vs *Greek* vocabularies, the *classicist* G. Nyström exercised an important influence in revealing to his Finnish compeers a new trail to the *Voyages d'Orient, a* tradition that had brought already from the 18th century many an architect and erudite from a number of European countries to Greece, Constantinople and the coasts of Ionia (i.e. English Society of the *Dilettanti*). Concomitantly, the magnificent volumes of *The Antiquities of Athens* were published by the painters and architects James Stuart and Nicholas Revett adding substantial information to the modern wanderers of the classical past (from 1762 to 1794).

1. *Stuart and Revett, drawing of the Acropolis and the Parthenon, view towards the east, 1751* (The Antiquities of Athens, *vol. II).*

1. Mentioned in Ville Lukkarinen, *Classicism and History; Anachronistic Architectural Thinking in Finland at the Turn of the Century-Jac. Ahrenberg and Gustaf Nyström*, Vammalan Kirjapaino Oy 1989, p. 35.

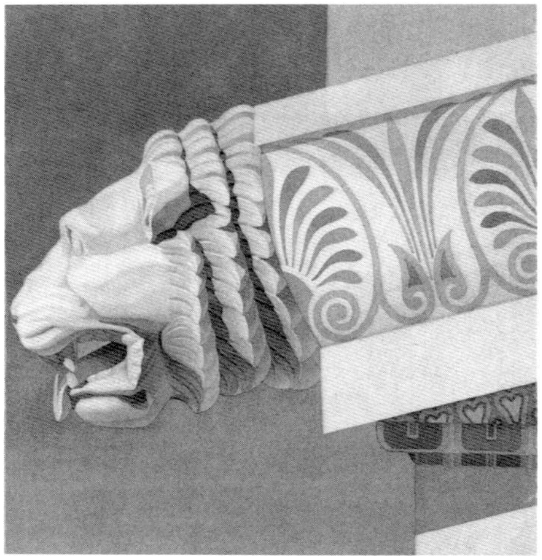

2. *Front page image of the catalogue of the 1982 exhibition* Paris-Rome-Athènes, *in Paris and Athens (Oct. 15 - Dec. 15, Alexander Soutzos National Gallery). Detail drawing from the Acropolis of Athens by Marcel Lambert (1877).*

It was mainly during the 19th century, following Greece's War of Independence (1821-1829) and the concurrent culmination of a romantic spirit of philhellenism, along with the rise of academic neo-classicism in Europe, that trips resumed at an accelerating pace aiming primarily at an *in situ* experience, study and restoration of Greek monuments. "Le XIXe siècle fut en Europe le siècle de la Grèce" wrote Olivier Picard, director of the École Française d'Athènes, in his prologue to the exhibition catalogue *Paris-Rome-Athènes, le voyage en Grèce des architectes français aux XIXe et XXe siècles.*[2]

2. This voluminous catalogue (1982) pays tribute to the young architects of the Villa Medicis in Rome, scholars of the *Académie de France*, re. École des Beaux-Arts/*Grands Prix de Rome* from 1845-1863 and well into the twentieth century, up to 1951!

FINNISH FORERUNNERS

Few Finnish architects attempted the study journey to Greece during the 19th century. One could for instance mention Jacob Ahrenberg (1847-1914), and before him, Georg Theodor Polychron Chiewitz (1815-1862). Chiewitz, though of Swedish origin, had lived and practiced architecture during the last active years of his life in Finland (Åbo, Helsingfors, 1851-1862).

The young Chiewitz spent two years in Greece (1834-1836) having been selected by his employer, railway engineer Adolf Eugène von Rosen, for his skills as an exceptional draftsman. Von Rosen had been commanded to participate in various naval-military re-organization works in Greece from October 1834 to July 1837, as agreed between the kings of Greece and Sweden. Chiewitz, who arrived in Greece while the archaeological excavations were just beginning on the Acropolis of Athens, produced among other things, drawings for defensive fortifications at the ports of Piraeus and Nafplion (the new country's capital from 1822 to 1834). During his stay in Greece, he also produced a series of fine acquarelles.[3]

3. *G.T.P. Chiewitz,* The Temple of Zeus and the Acropolis. Aten *(Acquarelle on paper, 1836-1837, Nationalmuseum, Stockholm).*

3. Chiewitz made acquarelles i.e. of the Fortress of Nafplion, and the Acropolis of Athens, nowadays housed at the National Museum of Stockholm. See Kursuppsatser 1987 GTP Chiewitz (1815-1862) *Tiden till 1850*, av Irma A. Hagström Bebyggelsehistoria med byggnadsvård. Stockholms Universitet, Institutionen för konstvetenskap.

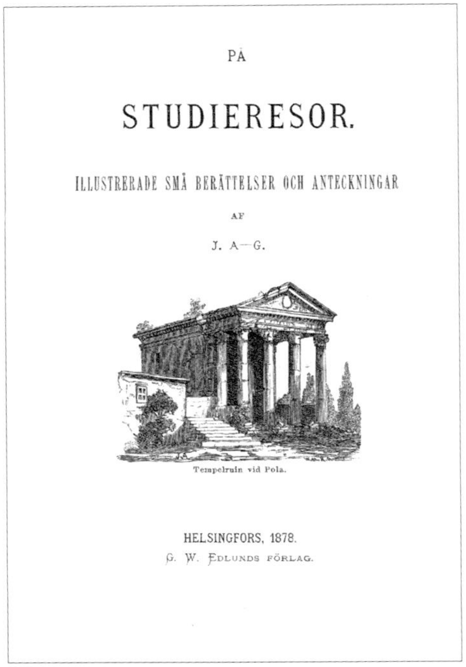

PÅ

STUDIERESOR.

ILLUSTRERADE SMÅ BERÄTTELSER OCH ANTECKNINGAR

AF

J. A—G.

Tempelruin vid Pola.

HELSINGFORS, 1878.

G. W. EDLUNDS FÖRLAG.

4. *J. Ahrenberg's* Carnet de Voyage, *1878.*

Jacob Ahrenberg is known to have travelled to Greece around 1875. Ahrenberg's architectural ideology, besides advocating a Finnish character in classicism, revolved at the same time around a strong belief in the romantic idea of an ethnic *characteristische*, an affinity to another, a regional, "Renaissance that suits our [Finnish] climate and has been adapted to it".[4] Already in his youth he was profoundly educated and proved to be an astute writer, expressing a form of poetic empathy that could easily compare to Göran Schildts' lyrical testimonies, written some 80 years later. In his travel notes, *På studieresor. Illustrerade små berättelser och anteckningar*, published in 1878 (Helsinfors, G.W. Edlunds Förlag), he provided a wonderful and detailed documentation of his journey to Greece.[5]

His first contact with this land, where ancient gods and muses excited his imagination, was from the sea. There, at the sight of Cythera, he expressed from a ship's deck the strength of his lyrical mind, and felt a genuine empathy for Greece's nature that had forged its cultural wealth for centuries:

> Eolus [Aeolus, the god of winds] stayed and he gave Cythera a new name "The Island of the Winds", when its beaches have never been calm, there are still storms. What would Vatteau[6] have said [...] with this background, more suitable for sea eagles and storm birds, than for the goddess of love [Aphrodite/Venus] and her blooming lusty fiddle, the sycamore trees, the pine trees, the laurels, the olives and the vines, everyone dreams of the storms, everyone clings anxiously to the roots.[7]

Still, gazing through islands of the Aegean, Melos, Paros, Antiparos, Syra -"the Queen of Cyclades", Cythnos, Ceos, Sounion, Egina, before finally setting foot in Piraeus:

> How many divine creations are still hidden under the Peneus River's mud, under Athens' streets, when such a treasure as this Venus [of Milos] has been preserved in an island, as poor, as unconventional as Melos.[8]
>
> To the right, Antiparos and Paros, whose snowy mountains to Greece's architects and sculptors, seem to be the shimmering substance for their ideals.[9]

In his thoughts when reaching Piraeus at an early morning hour, Ahrenberg revealed his expectations and esteem, exclaiming: "I knew this morning I would see the land of

---

4. Ville Lukkarinen, op. cit., p. 51.
5. op. cit., pp. 159-259.
6. Reference most probably to the 1717 painting *Pilgrimage to Cythera* by Jean-Antoine Watteau, perhaps as a criticism of its filling rococo scenery, as contrasted to the frugal and balanced harmony of the island's landscape.
7. V. Lukkarinen, op. cit., p. 160.
8. op. cit., p. 163.
9. op. cit., p. 164.

my dreams." He spent some time in Athens, being quite critical of the new city (*Det nya Athen*) and most particularly of Friedrich von Gärtner for his out-of-scale-and-mind palace for the newly installed King Otto of Greece [1836, nowadays housing the Greek Parliament]. According to Ahrenberg, "Gärtner planted the sampling of flinty and dry Berlin architecture in the Attic soil; it began to sprout and bear sad fruit as demonstrated by the royal palace of Athens, which vies with the Winter Palace in St Petersburg for the title of the ugliest royal palace in Europe. [...] And this in Greece, at the foot of the Acropolis!"[10]

Instead, he praised both Theophil Hansen's (1813-1891) and Ernst Ziller's (1837-1923) achievements, while also alluding to the negative side of some of Karl Friedrich Schinkel's ideas (1781-1841). As has been documented, the renowned Prussian classicist and exponent of the Greek Revival had suggested a sumptuous design for Otto's Palace on the emblematic rock of the Acropolis (1834), luckily unexecuted:

> You, honest Schinkel with your serious and well-constructed projects, you have better than all your fellow countrymen shown that the Greek forms belong to Greece, its nature, its climate, its fine material, [...] as it has been for these centuries valid and for which all these admirable forms were a true and necessary expression.[11]

5. *King Otto's Palace (upper right) by von Gärtner in 1873, around the time when Ahrenberg was in Athens. Today it houses the Greek Parliament.*

6. *Theophil Hansen's Greek Revival work in Athens: the Academy during construction (around 1860). At the bottom left stand Hansen and the young Ziller, supervising the work. (© NeoclassicalGreece.blogspot.gr)*

---

10. op. cit., pp. 174-175. Also mentioned by Timo Tuomi in a recent exhibition catalogue *Finnish Architects Gazing upon Greece; Sketches and Photographs*, edited by Maria Martzoukou, Jari Pakkanen and Timo Tuomi. Helsinki 2016, p. 14.

11. V. Lukkarinen, op. cit., p. 175.

7. *Aalto's sketch of the Lion Gate at Mycenae (1953)*

8, 9. *Sketches by Ahrenberg: The Propylaea at the Acropolis of Athens and the Lion Gate at Mycenae (1878).*

Ahrenberg's sketch of the Lion Gate made in 1878 demonstrates the slow progress of excavations, since the soil covering the lower part of the opening is at nearly the same level as it was in 1834 when painted by Edward Dodwell. Contrast this to the level depicted decades later, as for example in a sketch made by Aalto in 1953.

The most noteworthy side of Ahrenberg's journey had, however, to do with his experience of the ancient monuments, namely, old Athens (*Det gamla Athen*) and the Acropolis, its Roman monuments (*Romerska mines-märken i Athen*), and of the Peloponnese (*Från Athen till Epidauros. Från Epidauros till Argos, Mykene, till Korinth, från Korinth till Patras*). He left nineteenth-century Greece to travel to Saloniki, then still under Ottoman occupation, Constantinople (today Istanbul), Smyrna (today Izmir), and the Ionian Ephesus (today Efes).

Ahrenberg, overcome by the veiled melancholy[12] typical of nineteenth-century wanderers at the sight of fragments from the "birthplace of Western culture", produced a large group of fine etchings and sketches. In addition to his erudite knowledge of historians and geographers such as Herodotus and Thucydides, it is obvious from his writings that he was also aware of Pausanias' "oldest guide-book of the world".[13] His choices were also guided to a certain extent by his familiarity with Heinrich Schliemann and his excavations at Troy and Mycenae,[14] as well as with his acquaintance to Charles Garnier, laureate of the Prix de Rome from 1852-1853.

12. As a sign of Ahrenberg's feeling of melancholy, it is interesting to quote the caption he uses from Victor Hugo in his Studieresor notes: "Oh! que tout était grand dans cette époque antique! Si les ans n'avaient pas dévasté ce portique. Nous en retrouverions encore bien des lambeaux! Mais le temps, grand semeur de la ronce et du lierre, Touche les monuments d'une main familière. Et déchire le livre aux endroits les plus beaux!"

13. Pausanias, *Ελλάδος περιήγησις* or *Voyage historique de la Grèce* in the 1731 French translation.

14. Schliemann's excavations of 1874-76, with archaeologist Panayiotis Stamatakis, 30 years after Kyriakos Psistakis had found and restored the famous Lion Gate, following the description made many centuries before by Pausanias.

RESTORING THE CLASSICAL SPIRIT

A NEO-ROMANTIC SURGE

The turn to the twentieth century in Finland coincided with a spirit towards national independence and the expression of a national identity. The Finnish Pavilion designed by the young architects Geselius, Lindgren and Saarinen for the Paris World Expo in 1900 inaugurated, in a way, the move from an architectural standpoint. For a certain period during the two initial decades, architecture underwent a mixture of eclectic styles –from neo-gothic to Jugend and national romantic, to neo-classical– before opening to the venues of the modernist movement, prompted by technological and mechanization advancements, as well as by the Constructivist revolution– both sequels to the shift from the *individual* to the *collective*, to the fusion of art and industry, and to bursting socialist ideals. The advent of the Functionalist idea became the symbolic and practical vehicle to a modernist revival, as confused, illusory and one-sided the use of the terms *modern* and *functional* have proven to be when referring exclusively to the short interwar period.[15]

During the same time, Greece was torn apart as a result of consecutive wars which made the country at the beginning of the 1920s not any less "new" than Finland. By analogy to the latter, the development of a "new" Greece, nearly double in size, reclaiming national identity was then fluctuating between a revival of the spirit and cultural

10. *Finnish Pavilion at the World Expo in Paris 1900. Architects: Geselius, Lindgren and Saarinen.*

15. In accordance with the term "short" used by the historian Eric Hobsbawm indicating the century's brief timespan, as felt because of the successive upsets of wars and swift changes of different types (social, political, technological).

II. *The Greek Pavilion at the World Expo in Paris 1900. Architect: Lucien Magne. The pavilion was constructed of cast iron clad with stone tiles. It was an odd imitation of Byzantine church style which was also the choice of other Orthodox Balkan countries, as i.e. Serbia. The pavilion was moved to Athens and still operates as the Church of the Saviour (Aghios Sostis), alluding to the saving of King George I of Greece from an assassination attempt two years earlier.*

roots of Hellenism, of the frontier land Hellas at the threshold between East and West [re. the Classical and Byzantine heritage and the vernacular cultures of the mainland, the Aegean archipelago and the Ionian heritage of the East] on the one side, and on the other, a search for associations with the "modern" and the metaphorical and factual mutation of the "international" into something closer to the "national" or the "regional". Whichever differences there were, separating the aforementioned broad cultural trends, the modernist current in Greece was never quite dissociated from a Hellenic culture, loyal to ideas and values of man and society, and of time and place.

Although Ernest Renan's *Prière sur l'Acropole* was written almost half a century before (1865), its meaning and essence were brought forth to reawaken the conscience of a number of internationally famous men and women from the late 19th century onwards. Renan's romantic pronouncements were holding strong for the pure symbolism they carried:

> There is one and only one place in which perfection exists, and that is Athens, which outdid anything I had ever imagined [...] I had hitherto thought that perfection was not to be found in this world; one thing alone seemed to come anywhere near to perfection. [...] And now suddenly there arose [...] the Greek miracle [the Acropolis and the Parthenon].

In a comparable sense, expressing a sort of psychoanalytical contemplation as well as his incredulity, Sigmund Freud wrote:

> When finally, on the afternoon of our arrival, I stood on the Acropolis and cast my eyes around upon the landscape, a surprising thought suddenly entered my mind: 'So all this really does exist, just as we learnt at school!' [...] By the evidence of my

12. *Ernest Renan on the Acropolis. (Painting by André Brouillet. 1902)*

senses I am now standing on the Acropolis, but I cannot believe it [...] What I see here is not real [...] a feeling of de-realisation.[16]

Likewise, the dancer Isadora Duncan made Greece her home, settling in her "Mycenaean" stronghold in the Byron [Βύρων] suburb of Athens. Reminiscing on her long stay and career in the country, she retells her sense of awe at standing at the Propylaea of the Acropolis:

> As we climbed it seemed that all the life I had known until then stood out to me as a garment variegated, that I had never lived before, that I was born for the first time in this long breath of beauty, in this first contemplation. The sun rose behind the Pentelic, revealing his amazing clarity, the splendor of its marble sides which sparkled under the first rays of day. We climbed the last step of the Propylaea and we admired the temple shining in the morning light. By tacit agreement, we were staying silent, each of us was alone in front of Beauty! The time was too sacred to be expressed in words. It filled our hearts with a strange terror.[17]

The symbolic values expressed at the time by the revival of the humanistic spirit that ancient Greece represented in the eyes of erudites, artists and architects, both from the West and amongst Greeks, also had had practical effects. One instance was the revival of the modern Olympic Games in Athens (1896), after the efforts of Pierre Frédy,

13. *Isadora Duncan at the Propylaea of the Acropolis. (Photo taken in 1920 by Edward Steichen. Printed in 1981).*

16. Letter by Freud to Romain Rolland (1936) on his travels to Athens and visit to the Acropolis in 1904. See French translation of Freud's letter by Marlène Belilo, *Freud et ses voyages*, Michel de Maule, Paris, 2010, pp. 83-96.

17. Excerpt from Isadora Duncan's autobiography, *My Life* (1927) in which she recalls her family's arrival and stay in Greece in 1904.

Baron de Coubertin and of his Greek counterpart Dimitrios Vikelas. This important event strengthened even further the spiritual links between the international and the Greek communities and was a significant moral boost for the country.

Later in the 1920s, the revival of the *Delphic Idea*, the creation of the *Delphic Center* and the related international theater and dance festival by the Greek poet Angelos Sikelianos and his American wife Eva Palmer was another example. It was "an effort to bring forth [and convey] the spirit of classical tradition, which could also acquire a modern and oecumenical aspect".[18] According to Sikelianos' vision, Delphi was "this sacred site of the Ancient Amphictyonies,[19] a spiritual center to encourage and facilitate contact between scientists, artists and intellectual people from all countries".[20]

14. *The Panathenaic Olympic Stadium reconstructed on the site of the ancient one during the 4th quarter of the 19th cent. Architect Anastassis Metaxas. Here, Spyros Louis (1873-1940) enters the Stadium, winning the first Olympic Marathon race.*

15. *The 2nd Delphic Festival at the ancient Theater of Delphi (1930). Scene from Prometheus Bound of Aeschylus.*

18. An idea which had in fact aroused the interests (curiosity?) of an international élite in the 1920s and 30s; an idea aiming at reinstating a humanistic-holistic culture borrowed from unalienable principles of ancient Greek philosophy, in opposition to the rationalist trends of modern architecture and to eclectic functionalist dictates; as stated otherwise, the creation of the "Delphic Center" would "*encourage and facilitate contact between scientists, artists and intellectual people from all countries*." The *Delphic Idea* was masterminded by the national-romantic poet Angelos Sikelianos and supported by the architect Dimitris Pikionis.
It is worth noting that in the aftermath of war-torn Europe, several schemes aiming at the creation of such "spititual arks" concentrating and making accessible humanity's knowledge (see La Bibliothèque Interrnationale) and providing new philosophical perspectives to human life, were proposed or even applied in Europe, albeit in rather utopian scales. Examples could refer to Paul Otlet's Palais Mondial-Mundaneum (to which Le Corbusier was involved in proposing his unlimited growth establishments/museums. See http://mundaneum.be). Reference could also include the proposal of a Centre Mondial de Communication by the sculptor Hendrik Christian Andersen and the architect Ernest Hébrard (later Professor at the N.T.U. of Athens), the Mediterranean Academy of Erich Mendelsohn and Amédée Ozenfant, Rudolf Steiner's Goetheanum, etc. On this matter see: Kostas Tsiambaos' recent treatise: *Αμφίθυμη νεωτερικότητα .../ Ambivalent modernism; 9+1 texts on modern architecture in Greece*. Publ. Επίκεντρο 2017, pp. 80-97.

19. Amphictyony: an association of neighboring states in ancient Greece to defend a common religious center; broadly, an association of neighboring states for their common interest. See definition by Merriam-Webster Dictionary.

20. A. Sikelianos, *Γράμματα/Letters*, vol. A, p. 151, also mentioned by K. Tsiambaos op. cit., p. 60.

16. *The Ilissos River with the Acropolis of Athens in the background (photo by Fréderic Boissonnas, 1910).*

17. *Charles-Édouard Jeanneret (Le Corbusier) on the Acropolis of Athens (photo by Auguste Klipstein. 1911).*

As will be later assessed, Alvar Aalto came back and became nearly obsessed with the idea of "centers of exchange", that is of intra- and inter-cultural exchanges, reflected in the *Delphic Idea* and its Delian analogy.

In spite of rather limited study trips to Greece during the two troubled and unstable decades at the beginning of the century, exemplified mainly by the Finnish architect and teacher Usko Nyström in 1905, the Swiss photographer François-Fréderic Boissonnas between 1907 and 1919,[21] Charles-Édouard Jeanneret (Le Corbusier) in 1911,[22] and the British journalist Robert Smythe Hichens around 1912,[23] there was a new wave of individual travelers from 1922 onwards.

21. François-Fréderic Boissonnas, *L'image de la Grèce et de la Serbie. Photos.* Texts by W. Deonna, G. Arvanitakis and D. Baud-Bovy, Paris, Jean Budry [c. 1935].

22. Charles-Édouard Jeanneret-Le Corbusier, *Voyage d'Orient, 1910-1911.*

23. Robert Smythe Hichens, *The Near East Dalmatia, Greece and Constantinople*, London, Hodder and Stoughton, 1913.

CLOSER TO ALVAR AALTO'S *EARLY YEARS*

Finnish architects, including Usko Nyström (1861-1925) and Hilding Ekelund (1893-1984) were among those who resumed their trips to Greece from the eve of the twentieth century onwards, seeking to acquaint themselves with ancient and contemporary Greece.

Usko Nyström, an influential teacher of both Eliel Saarinen and Alvar Aalto at the Helsinki Technical University, visited Greece in 1905. Although not quite a "classicist" himself, he had nevertheless acquired an all-around knowledge of the Medieval and Classical periods, which he taught as one of his major educational themes. At a time when the Beaux-Arts School was still encouraging young architects to study ancient monuments, Nyström, though an "anti-monumentalist" rejecting academicism, might have been influenced accordingly during his one-year stage there. His short stay in Paris was perhaps the reason for his acquaintance with the French archaeologist Gaston Deschamps (1861-1931), whom he quoted in a brief account of his trip to Greece (*Från en sommartripp till Grekland.* Arkitekten, Januari 1906, pp. 6-10). Having returned to Finland from Paris, he might have also been informed about Deschamps' book *La Grèce d'aujourd'hui*, published shortly after.[24]

While in Greece (July-August 1905), Nyström was not only attracted by the monuments and ruins on the Acropolis of Athens, Acrocorinth and/or Olympia, but also by the land, sea, and not least, the people and artefacts. He wrote about his experience

18. *Usko Nyström drew himself sitting on the capital of a Doric column (1905).*

24. Gaston Deschamps, *La Grèce d'aujourd'hui*, Paris, Armand Colin et Cie. Éditeurs, 1894.

19. *The six hours that Nyström spent at the harbor of Corfu in July 1905 during a stopover in his passage from Italy to Athens were characterized as "the most enjoyable during his whole trip".*

with an eye surveying and permeating the natural topography and the variation of its profile, its elements and alternate colors:

> I would like to feel with my fingers [placed] on this nature, which had a significant share in the culture and art of which we were able to follow the clear and transparent tracks all the way to this day. [...] A full day, between Patras and Athens, you can be enchanted by the iridescent and shining color scheme of the Korinthian Bay's spikes [mountain peaks], sparkling sunny breezes, [...] perhaps the only thing you see all day against a rug as warm blue and intensely brilliant as you did not even imagine in your dreams, and behind, the rewarding gaze of Parnassos, Kithairon's calm, imposing masses. Mountains are visible to you, far away and yet so close, in the clear, clean air, shining and glowing in fine blue and violet shifts, harmonious and translucent [...] At such moments, when the eye is stuck in the intricate, yet harmonious color contours of the landscape, when the womb and life are as blown away, and the blood begins to flow faster in your veins, you feel at ease, singular and lively, maybe at a moment, thanks heaven, which did not make you painter, in order to lure you into a vain attempt of fixing a mood, volatile like the wind, varied like the pictures in a kaleidoscope or color shades.
>
> Volatile impressions of nature and people [...] full of all sorts of tourist charms: oriental carpets, pipes, slippers, fustanellas, shoes with crochet tips, column bits, fake bronzes and clay jars. And how could I not despise these modern vandals [...] loathing and biting away valuable historical monuments to their remote countries! That's why I took with me only a tiny piece of the shell limestones' period of which the Zeus Temple in Olympia was built, laying there loose on the soil.[25].

20. *Usko Nyström's sketch from Olympia (1905). It brings to mind an almost similar rendering drawn by Alvar Aalto more than 50 years later.*

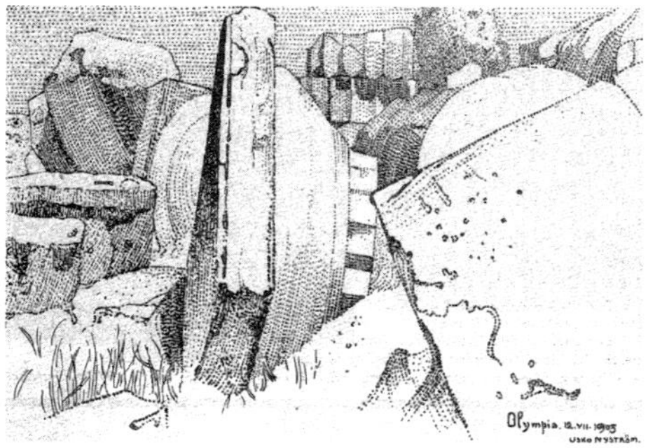

25. Usko Nyström *Från en sommartripp till Grekland.* Arkitekten, Januari 1906. See also Ranska Eija on *Usko Nyström*, Suomen Arkkitehtuurimuseon historiallista julkaisuja, Helsinki 2014, pp. 92-96. In his contepmtuous stand against *these modern vandals [...] loathing and biting away valuable historical monuments to their remote countries!* Nyström reiterates indeed Lord Byron's verses *Dull is the eye that will not weep to see | Thy walls defaced, thy mouldering shrines removed | By British hands, which it had best behoved* published some 100 years earlier (from Byron's *Childe Harold's Pilgrimage*, Canto XV. Publ. 1812-1818).

Nyström carried with him impressions, unique for their genuine appreciation and utterance, different in spirit from those which he had experienced and expressed during his previous trips (i.e. Italy). Aspects of them were recorded through the remarkable *pointilliste* sketches he produced and later published in his own country. Was his contemporary Paul Signac an acquaintance, or had he rather been of some influence?

Five years older than his homologue Alvar Aalto, and like him a "radical reformer" (re. Vilhelm Helander), Georg Hilding Ekelund (1893-1984) and his wife and partner Eva Kuhlefelt (1892-1984) approached Greece from the East, aboard a ship from Smyrna (today Izmir) in November of 1926. Ekelund had travelled to Italy a bit earlier (1921-1922), following what was at the time a *sine qua non* destination for Finnish and Swedish architects. Aalto followed suit in 1924. In this respect, it is interesting to note that in the text of the Museum of Finnish Architecture announcing the exhibition of Hilding Ekelund's architecture in 2012, while there was a fairly proportionate mention of the architect's trip to Italy, his trip to Greece and to Hellenic sites in Ionia were surprisingly omitted.

As in the case of Alvar Aalto, Ekelund as well as other young Finnish architects sought to be directly associated with the work of Swedish colleagues, exponents of pure early forms of the so-called *Nordic Classicism* (re. Gunnar Asplund, Sven Markelius, Hakon Ahlberg and Ivar Tengbom). This tradition could have in fact justified the traveler-wanderer Hilding Ekelund's expectations for undertaking the classic voyage, namely to Greece.

He was already quite well acquainted with the sites in the many places he visited, partly through his architectural studies at the Helsinki Technical University ten years earlier, partly through the relevant literature, and partly from his inclination to the prevalent architectural style in the 1920s, before the advent of *Functionalism* towards the end of the decade. Moreover, during his studies, as well as Aalto's, Banister Fletchers' *History of Architecture on the Comparative Method* (1896) and Auguste Choisy's *Histoire de l'Architecture* (1899) were emblematic documents in architectural education. Both were important references to the principles and realizations of classical and other historical paradigms in most countries, including in Finland; for many, they continued to be in subsequent decades, up to the 1960s!

Hilding Ekelund was thus more than an adequate recipient of a classical education. His broad view on the cultural dimension of architecture in place and time, coincided and perhaps was also boosted by another, also unique, trip to picturesque Greece. It was few years before his trip to Greece that the German photographer Hans Holdt (1887-1944) and the Austrian novelist-essayist Hugo von Hofmannsthal (1874-1929) had published their magnificent volume *Griechenland. Baukunst, Landschaft und Volksleben*, describing and illustrating with exceptional photographs their experience throughout the whole of Greece. Already from their introduction, they had expressed it in such a compassionate way that for any reader of that time, Greece would seem as the ideal spiritual destination for erudites, naturalists and architects alike:

21, 22. *The Acropolis of Athens and the Temple of Apollo in Delphi, early 1920s, (photos by Hans Holdt and Hugo von Hofmannsthal,* Griechenland. Baukunst, Landschaft und Volksleben*).*

> Of all the journeys, that to Greece is the most spiritual. [...] Ours was a spiritual pilgrimage, and we had forgotten that from this landscape might emanate another perfume than that of memories alone. [...] The first impression of this landscape is stern [...] It casts off all dreamy visions, be they historical or otherwise. It is dry, close-fisted, expressive, and strange as a fearful emaciated countenance. But on it shines a light the like of which the eye has never seen before, a light that fills it with such joy that it would seem the eye had first learnt the meaning of seeing today [...] This light is at the same time inexpressibly mild. It shows up clearly the slightest detail with such distinctness [...] It can only be compared with spirit. Things must exist thus in a wonderful intellect, so wakeful and so restful, so set apart, so joined [...] And, indeed, in this light the spiritual is more embodied, and the physical more spiritualized than elsewhere in the world.[26]

Prior to their expedition to Greece, the Ekelunds had already visited ancient Hellenic sites in Anatolia (Ephesus, Priene, Miletos, November 22-23, 1926). Aside from taking analytical notes, the modern travelers were also apparently equipped with the latest *Baedeker*-Greece, which had last appeared in its 4th edition in 1909 (at first in 1889). Unlike others among his professional peers, Ekelund produced only a negligible token of sketches unrelated to ancient sites. Instead, he used extensively his photographic apparatus, taking *instantanés* shots for future reference.

Did this explain his nature as an "ordinary" traveler, a wanderer, or a "vagabond", one taking avid pleasure in just seeing things of all sorts, as many as possible, in the course of prolonged *architectural promenades* in the broadest sense, including people, their life modes (*genres de vie* as coined by early 20th century social geographers, such as i.e. Vidal de la Blache), their habitats, and the landscapes surrounding ancient monuments? As Helander emphatically notes:

> Ekelund [...] acquainted himself with it [the architecture of the Mediterranean] at its roots, and undoubtedly the most thoroughly of all Finnish architects [...] What was new [...] was an interest not so much in great monuments as in the cultural landscape, ordinary urban structure and the timeless everyday living environment.[27]

Furthermore in a similar spirit, Björn Forsén and Erkki Sironen observed that:

> As a traveler, Hilding Ekelund was an observant private person on an adventurous trip, a vagabond, but at the same time a professional architect on study trip [...] It

26. Hans Holdt and Hugo von Hofmannsthal, *Griechenland. Baukunst, Landschaft und Volksleben*. Publisher Ernst Wasmuth A.G., Berlin 1923, pp. V-VIII. The book was also part of the collection of the Finnish-Swedish Art Historian Osvald Sirén (1879-1966). Sirén's copy of the book can nowadays be found at the University Library of Helsinki/ Kaisatalo.

27. Vilhelm Helander, *Hilding Ekelund in the Vanguard of Finnish Architecture*, in: *Hilding Ekelund (1893-1984) Architect*. Monograph by the Museum of Finnish Architecture. Vammalan Kirjapaino oy, 1997, p. 45.

23, 24, 25. *Hilding Ekelund's photos: panoramic view of Athens; the Erechtheion on the Acropolis; and an early Doric column in Olympia (Archives of the Museum of Finnish Architecture).*

26. *Albert Tournaire's restoration of Delphi according to the existing ruins at the time (1894).*

> was a picturesque journey [in Greece], a journey of architectural interest in the buildings and culture, and where the vagabond was interested in the picturesque and everyday life, men and their hardships and social life.[28]

The trip to Greece lasted for a short month. In Athens, Ekelund stayed for almost two weeks, during which he visited the Acropolis three times (Dec. 1, 4 and 8, 1926). With the city as a base, he also visited the nearby resorts of Eleusis, Cape Sounion and Piraeus. From Athens, he then traveled through Nea and Palea Corinth, Kharvati, Mycenae, Nafplion, Tiryns, Argos, Tripolis, Sparta, Mistra, Megalopolis, Andristsaina, Bassae, Kalamata, Kyparissia, and Olympia to Patras. From there he took a ship to Brindisi on December 21, 1926. In addition to these destinations, Hilding Ekelund also tried to get to Delphi with a steam boat from Piraeus. This trip was canceled due to lack of time.

On several occasions, Ekelund had kept personal notes of his experience which indicate the extent of his cultivated eye and mind. He described his visit to the Acropolis as if holding a cinematographic camera in addition to his photographic apparatus, following his gaze and movement through the site:

> There everything stands as it stands. In the top right, Nike Aptero's little graceful sanctuary hovered, to the left is Agrippa's Roman harsh posture, right in front, the

---

28. Björn Forsén and Erkki Sironen (eds), *Det svunna Grekland; Finska reses-kildringar från tiden före massturismen*. Svenska litteratursällskapet i Finland, Oy Nord Print Ab, Helsingfors 2006, p. 230.

> Propylaea opens its asymmetrical bosom to the visitor. Solemnly trains your gaze between the portraits' splendid ionic columns, and the plateau opens in front of a free-spirited design.[29]

Even three decades after returning to Finland, Ekelund kept making references to both the cultural and the natural landscape of Greece, such as in his inaugural speech at the Technical University of Helsinki:

> You find in yourself a yearning for the cool, fresh, natural water bubbling out through an unspoilt spring [...] Or perhaps the crystal-clear stream that starts in the mountains surrounding the Apollo-Epicurus temple in Phigalia [Bassae] of Peloponnesus, and reappears, cool and refreshing, at the innumerable wells in the squares and gardens of a small town called Andritsaina. This is the kind of longing the townsman feels in his well-planned town flat when he thinks of the countryside and its natural charm.

Illustrating this lecture, Ekelund made use of slides which provided ample proof of his all-round and thorough education in ancient Greece most particularly including Choisy's plan of the Acropolis, Albert Tournaire's perspective restauration of the sanctuary and site of Delphi, etc.[30]

---

29. op. cit., p. 236.

30. *Hilding Ekelund (1893-1984) Architect.* Monograph by the Museum of Finnish Architecture. Vammalan Kirjapaino Oy, 1997, p. 258. Also in Timo Tuomi's "The Call of the Mediterranean; Hilding Ekelund's great Journeys of the 1920s", op. cit., pp. 77-79. The typed manuscript of Ekelund's speech is part of the collection and accessible from the Archives of the Museum of Finnish Architecture in Helsinki.

1933. ALVAR AALTO'S FIRST TRIP TO GREECE

THE 4th CIAM CONGRESS

Like the enigmas of an ancient myth, Alvar Aalto left a rather imperceptible though also paradoxically discernible trail of his hurried passage through Greece. His traverse is marked by rather limited factual events during his two visits, in 1933 and twenty years later, in 1953.[31]

What had Aalto sought to "see" in Greece? What had he "seen" and what could he have "seen" but failed to "see", either by idiosyncrasy, or choice, by omission or unawareness? What did his Greek contemporaries "see" in him and through him? What influence has Aalto had in their architectural vision and work?

Episodes in erudites' or geniuses' lives have often been subjected to credible interpretations affording some degree of supposition and abstraction. The fact that Aal-

---

31. A mistaken date for Alvar Aalto's first trip to Greece should be brought to the reader's attention. In Göran Schildt's book *Alvar Aalto skisser*, published by Söderström in 1973, the preface ("Förord", p. 9) attributes its occurrence in 1929 along with the *CIAM Congress* (?). The sketches that Aalto made at Delphi, Olympia, Mycenae and Mykonos which follow Aalto's texts in the same publication are also wrongly attributed as having been drawn in 1929, instead of the actual date 1953! As has been documented, the 2nd CIAM of 1929 was held in Frankfurt. This mistake remains therefore as a riddle asking for an explanation. Was it Aalto's absent-mindedness or lack of interest or memory concerning mistaken dates, when already in his 70s? Was it perhaps Schildt's lack of appropriate attention in checking the accuracy of references provided during discussions with his good friend? Or even, could it solely be an oversight during the editing-printing process? In any case, in the mind of the present essay's author, the issue lingers as a mystery, the size of which is irrelevant to that of two great men.

UUSI SUOMI

TOIMITUS: Ruoholahdenkatu 21 C, 00180 Helsinki 18 • Puhelin (vaihde) 647 711
Avoinna kello 9.00—01.00 (sunnuntaisin kello 16.00—01.00)

Päätoimittajat: Johannes Koroma (vastaava), Juha Numminen, Jyrki Haikonen. Toimituspäälliköt: Jaakko Korjus (hallinto), Jyrki Vesikansa (uutiset), Veli-Antti Savolainen (viikonvaihde). Uutispäällikkö: Mikko Hietala. Ulkoasu: Matti Lukkari. Apulaisuutispäälliköt: Eero Lehtinen, Tom Kallma, Nils Rosberg. Toimitussihteerit: Sirpa Kivistö, Aarne Nurmi, Christian Sjöstedt, Olavi Tanner, Kauko Wäyrynen. Osastopäälliköt: Heikki Eteläpää (kulttuuri), Heikki Korpinen (politiikka), Heikki Liljeström (ulkomaat), Juhani Melart (urheilu), Timo Vuorio (talous).

Sunnuntaina, 19. pnä maaliskuuta 1978

Jyväskylä tekee tietä moottoritielle

Alvar Aallon taloja haloiksi

• Alvar Aallon varhaistyö sijaitsee kunniakkaalla paikalla vastapäätä Taulumäen kirkkoa. Liikenne vain häiritsee kuolemaksi saakka.

• Jyväskylä on ainoa kaupunki maailmassa, missä voidaan nähdä arkkitehti Alvar Aallon suunnittelemia rakennuksia aina 1920-luvulta kuluvan vuosikymmenen viimeisimpiin saavutuksiin asti.
Toistaiseksi.

• Minnekään näitä rakennuksia ei enää tule lisää, mutta Jyväskylässä on jo vedetty punakynää kartalla arkkitehdin varhaistöiden päälle.
Taulumäentie ykkösessä nököttävää omakotitaloa kiskotaan nyt kaikista nurkista.

— Ei Aallon nimeä häpäise se, että yksi talo pistetään haloiksi, väittää Keski-Suomen museon johtaja Sirkka Valjakka. — Talohan ei ole edes arkkitehtonisesti merkittävä.

— Vanhat talot eivät ole aina mitä tahansa vanhoja taloja, sanoo puolestaan kustannustoimittaja Jussi Jäppinen, joka on ahkerasti kantanut korsia kekoon mm. inventoimalla Jyväskylän säilyttämisen arvoiset rakennukset. — Vanhoilla rakennuksilla on selviä kytkentöjä toisiinsa.

— Niiden arvoa voisi mitata rahassakin: Aallon yhtenäinen tuotanto olisi melkoinen matkailuvaltti.

Taloa ei suinkaan aiota purkaa huvin vuoksi. Entistä ehompi nelostie tulee kulkemaan Taulumäen kirkon edestä ja sen alle jää neljä taloa. Näistä kolme on rakennettu Alvar Aallon vaikutuksesta.

Sirkka Valjakan mielestä on turha nostaa haloota enää, kun valtuusto on tehnyt purkamisesta päätöksen.

— Mikael silloin oteta innos-

• Jyväskylän vanha sähkölaitos on yksi Jyväskylän kolmesta kansallisromanttisesta rakennuksesta. Jussi Jäppisen maalaama rakennus puretaan vielä tänä vuonna ratapihan laajennuksen tieltä.

27, 28, 29. *Houses by Aalto from the early 1920s: those slated for demolition (left and upper right), and Karpio's summer villa in Jyvaskyla (1923) (lower right) (front page of Uusi Suomi newspaper from the KX archive, and photos by K. Xanthopoulos, 1978).*

to never kept a diary during his many journeys abroad has been an impediment to acquiring adequate evidence. For his mnemonic recollections he at first resorted to photography by selecting his themes rather deliberately. Later, through his sketches, he was using his *thinking hand*[32] as if willing himself to fathom the meaning, form and structure of what he saw, both in nature and in artefacts, as cultural and spiritual. Thus, the story relating Aalto to Greece and vice-versa could be constructed on valid approximations of a fictive nature that would complement the few facts and traces left by the Finnish master; trailing Ariadne's tattered, and nowadays indeed inconspicuous thread!

Approximations could however elucidate the nature of less visible "trails" as to the architect's idiosyncrasy and "anarchism" [*αναρχία* meaning 'leaderlessness', 'lack of rules'], and his eclectic choices in seeking personal contacts, more or less known and recorded in some of his articles and letters, as well as in countless critical publications from the 1920s onwards.

32. Paraphrasing Juhani Pallasmaa's "The Thinking Hand".

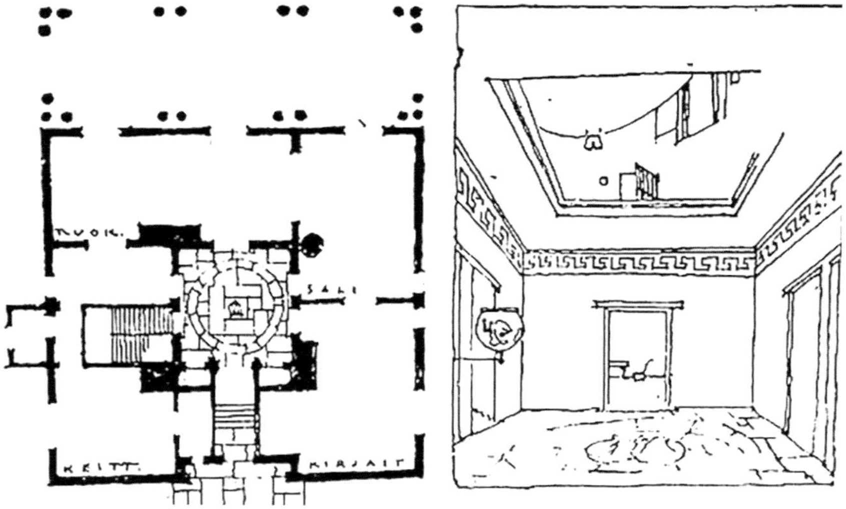

30. *Aalto's early drawing for his brother's house "Casa Väino" in Alajärvi (1925) exemplifies the architect's vision of the classical Mediterranean atrium. Though mostly covered for climatic reasons, its important role was extended in various configurations and scales in many of his subsequent projects, as a nodal space assembling people and connecting adjoining spaces of a variety of forms and functions.*
The atrium [αίθριον/aethrion in its Greek etymological root] appeared in Greece as an essential element to the disposition of spaces (i.e. house types in ancient Olynthos, Delos, Priene, Athens). It is present even today in modern Greek houses, where most of "life is lived in the open-air", as Dimitri Pikionis and Aris Konstantinidis were often pointing out.
Aalto, being influenced mainly from the Italian paradigm (i.e. Pompeii), was perhaps also aware of its initial origin (for an excellent overview see: Venierakis, Manolis, Atrium + Housing, *Department of Architectural Engineering - Democritus University of Thrace DUTH - October 2013).*

Alvar Aalto followed a more or less established tradition common to most of his Finnish predecessors.

First, a considerable part of his education had to do with ancient Greek history, architecture and art, in addition to the Renaissance period. Many quotes by himself and symbolic references and metaphors by other scholars attest to this fact:[33]

> I've been going hard at the art of ancient Crete and Mycenae for the last couple of weeks, morning to night. Such exciting subjects just won't let you go once you start studying them. (Alvar Aalto, 1916)
>
> We are flying in bright sunshine - the first Hellenic day of my life.[34]

Then, there was also the tradition of reaching out to the prominent Swedish classicists (Gunnar Asplund, Sven Markelius etc.). For Aalto, getting trainee job experience near Gunnar Asplund already in 1920 was an objective related in the young man's mind to the "unconventional revival of the Classical heritage".[35] The fact that Asplund had adopted "ways for fusing the vernacular and classicism and for bridging the gap between Nordic and Mediterranean worlds", might have also been an important motivation for Aalto's attraction.[36]

---

33. i.e. from Göran Schildt, William Curtis, Demetri Porphyrios, et al.
34. From Alvar Aalto's letter to Ragnar Ypyä, 1923.
35. Göran Schildt, *Alvar Aalto; The Early Years*, Otava Publ., Helsinki 1984, p. 160.
36. William Curtis, *Modern Architecture since 1900*, 3rd edition, Phaidon 1996, p. 146.

Influences were relatively apparent in Aalto's early works which adopted a sort of *classical-vernacular* idiom (i.e. in Jyväskylä, Seinäjoki, Alajärvi, and elsewhere).

The third tradition which Aalto was to follow soon after had to do with traveling to the Mediterranean south, and especially to Italy (from 1924). Fostered by his teacher of the Italian Renaissance Armas Lingren, he had built an *a priori* admiration for Brunelleschi, Alberti, Palladio, and Venetian architecture, for their "synthetic landscape" and the "rising towns" of Tuscany; not less, an equal admiration for those medieval towns usually perched on the hilltops of the undulating idyllic landscape (i.e. San Gimigniano). The unique natural and man-made environment of the Italian paradigm justified the magnetic force exercised in Aalto's imagination and perception for what he had deemed as the uttermost in culture and harmony.

The proofs were there to boost mimetic adaptations! As Shildt points out, Aalto's admiration for Italy, "became particularly real for him when he moved to Jyväskylä, facetiously known as 'the Athens of Finland'. After his trip to Italy in 1924, Aalto would have liked to see it as 'the Florence of Finland', and he entered heart and soul into the task of giving Jyväskylä an Italian touch".[37]

The rich cultural heritage of legendary Italy had retained its full physical presence and integrity, its obvious charm and power of seduction, being time- and space-wise closer than the more distant history and geography of Greece. At the time, Greece's monuments and "ruins" were less of a choice for Nordic architects. Their cultural imprint and oecumenical value, fostered more a sense of spiritual contemplation, ethical respect and introspection, than an immediate response by and through the senses. In the Italian trip, the "reality" was closer to imagining the "metaphor". In the Greek trip, the "metaphor" was an enigmatic riddle in connection to "reality". A riddle that in a way was candidly expressed, for instance by Freud's "incredulity" and "doubt" for a supposed "déjà-vu", and by Charles-Édouard Jeanneret's crushing sense, his *écrasement*, where ruins eluded his mind and understanding, while facing the Acropolis of Athens for the first time.[38]

Besides considerations as the above, it is meaningful to mention that travelling to Greece and to the south-east Mediterranean in the 1920s was not quite an easy under-

31. *Aalto's sketch from a trip to San Gimigniano in 1948 (source: Schildt G. (ed.), 1978,* Sketches: Alvar Aalto, *London & Cambridge (Mass): MIT Press).*

32. *Partial view of San Gimigniano (photo by K. Xanthopoulos. © KX Archive 2017).*

37. G. Schildt, op. cit., p. 252.

38. Le Corbusier's exclamation: "Voir l'Acropole [...] Le grand coup a été le premier. Admiration, adoration, puis écrasement. Ça fuit, ça m'échappe". In *Le Voyage d'Orient* [1966], Marseille, Parenthèses; 1987, pp. 158-168. The impulsive reaction of the architect in view of the Acropolis monuments could be compared to similar, though more poetic, references vis-à-vis man's feelings when confronted with "beauty" in general. See for instance Charles Baudelaire's pathetic verse: "Ah! faut-il éternellement souffrir, ou fuir éternellement le beau?" (Le spleen de Paris, 1869), or Paul Valéry's dialogue between Phaidros and Eupalinos: "Ce qu'il y a de plus beau est nécessairement tyrannique" (Eupalinos, ou l'architecte, 1921).
In contrast, Alvar Aalto took a rather contemplative stance, observing the Acropolis monuments at a slow pace in the course of two consecutive mornings in 1933.

33, 34. *The tower hill-towns of Vatheia and Flomochori in the Peloponnese. Hilding Ekelund did not get to visit these unique towns although he had travelled as far down as Kalamata, the main city of the Mani peninsula. Neither did Alvar Aalto, as his southernmost destination during his 2nd trip in 1953 was Olympia (photos by K. Xanthopoulos. © KX Archive 1976).*

taking. As Timo Tuomi had pointed out, it was in fact "very difficult" and any "architectural enthusiast had to be decisive, patient and content with very little in order to reach his goal. Often it was necessary to walk or ride long distances to reach ruins."[39] However, there were such wanderers with vigorous stamina even in those times; wanderers and "vagabonds" such as the young Ekelunds for instance, and many more before and after, who had the will, the capability and enough time to fulfill the scope of their travel ambitions.

Was Alvar Aalto in the position to fulfill his?

At the time when he had decided to expand his travelling vistas beyond Italy and other countries that he had been visiting for almost a decade, his first trip to Greece was already constrained by the availability of time and by the scope for its attainment. In 1933, he had already proved of his creative versatility having moved in no time from his classical phase to the functionalist innovation. His skill in interpreting *Funkis* architecture was demonstrated in an impressive professional roster. He was involved in numerous competitions and had achieved a number of projects of international acclaim: the Viipuri City Library (competition 1927 and final version 1933), the Turun Sanomat

39. Timo Tuomi, op. cit., p. 16.

building (1928), the Paimio tuberculosis sanatorium (1929-1932),[40] and many more. Before moving his office from Turku to Helsinki (1933), Aalto was already very busy and the pressure of time was weighing heavily upon him. He therefore had to tailor his trip carefully and find specific reasons that could match his intellectual interests as well as his ambitions for international recognition. On the other hand, Finland was already too "small" for the architect's call, and for his need to establish contacts with an active élite well beyond his country's borders.

It is in this context that Aalto had decided his first trip to Athens in late July 1933.

The primary motivation for his short visit and nominal participation during the last phases of the 4th CIAM Congress originated at first from a cause nearer to his ambitions than to his spiritual affinities and needs.

As is known, the Congress was to deal with the "Functional City". The Greek delegates were in favor of using instead the term "Organic City/Η οργανική πόλις".[41] A related quote to a "biology of the world" was in fact spelled out a bit earlier by Le Corbusier when standing in front of the 33 city plans prepared for the Congress.[42]

The debates between *functional* and *organic* were in a way indicating the subtle differences of expressed views leaning towards either a settled doctrine and a corollary fragmentation into broad functional entities, or to more flexible and holistic approaches to city growth and form. The related dilemmas expressed during the 4th Congress had set a stigma for what in fact comprised, a ceaseless issue in modern architecture and urban planning and design. The same dilemmas were reasons inciting Le Corbusier to refer to the arguments set during the Congress as "constatations" instead of the more deterministic "résolutions", which were the Congress's goal from the start. It is certain that these issues were among Aalto's central concerns and could have meant a significant impetus to his increased and substantial participation in a Congress, which his critic and theoretical mentor Sigfried Giedion had later judged as "the longest, most exciting, and most fruitful of the CIAM congresses".[43]

Aalto had already been present and apparently quite active in the previous 2nd CIAM Congress held in Frankfurt (1929). He was then a newly-appointed national representative of Finland and had met with a number of prominent figures (Giedion, Gropius,

35. *Turun Sanomat, main entrance staircase, (photo by K. Xanthopoulos. © KX Archive 1965).*

36. *Paimio Sanatorium, partial view (photo by K. Xanthopoulos. © KX Archive 1965).*

---

40. The Paimio Sanatorium was the subject of an open competition with 13 entries submitted Jan. 31, 1928-1929, basic design phase completed in Spring 1930, and with supplementary drawings until 1932.

41. i.e. by Dimitri Pikionis in a critical essay "Γύρω από ένα Συνέδριο/Around a Congress", in 1933, in *D. Pikionis, Κείμενα/Texts*, MIET Publ., 1985, pp. 168-170.

42. Mentioned in Eric Mumford, *The CIAM Discourse on Urbanism, 1928-1960*. The MIT Press paperback ed., 2002, p. 79. On the same issue, see also a recent article by Lina Dima, "'Η 'Οργανική Πολις' του 4ου CIAM και ο Ιωάννης Δεσποτόπουλος/The 'Organic City' of the 4th CIAM and Ioannis Despotopoulos", in *Ελληνική Αρχιτεκτονική στον 20ό και 21ο αιώνα· Ιστορία-Θεωρία-Κριτική/Greek Architecture in the 20th and 21st centuries; History-Theory-Criticism*, ed. Andreas Giacumacatos, Gutenberg, 2016, pp. 74-76.

43. S. Giedion, *Space, Time and Architecture*, 5th edition, March 1970. Cambridge Mass., Harvard University Press. p. 699.

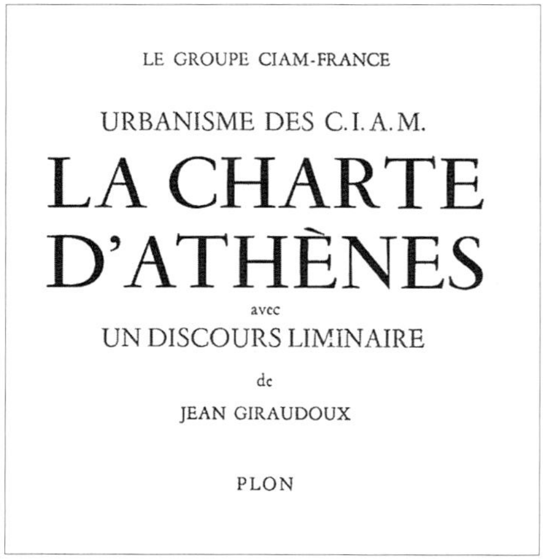
LE GROUPE CIAM-FRANCE

URBANISME DES C.I.A.M.

LA CHARTE D'ATHÈNES

avec

UN DISCOURS LIMINAIRE

de

JEAN GIRAUDOUX

PLON

37. *1942. Jose Luis Sert's book based on the "constatations" of the 4th CIAM of 1933 in Athens.*

38. *1943. Ten years after the 4th CIAM, Le Corbusier incorporated the same "constatations" to compose his doctrinary* La Charte d'Athènes. *(First published in 1943 in Paris by Plon). A second publication (by Minuit) followed in 1947 bearing the weight of Le Corbusier's signature.*
In the first publication, Jean Giraudoux wrote his poetic "Discours luminaire" starting with a visionary and emblematic prologue:
"Ne parlons pas du ciel, pour lequel la méthode ne souffre pas de conteste, Mais chaque homme possédant la Terre, chaque citoyen possédant son pays au même titre que tous les autres hommes et citoyens, il n'est pas de politique humaine et nationale que dans l'ambition de lui rendre et facile et réel l'exercice de cette égalité."

Stam, Neutra, Breuer, Lurçat, etc.), with the exception of the most influential of all, the absent Le Corbusier. The presence of this elite of modern architecture was attractive to Aalto, as was the Congress' main themes revolving around the "minimum dwelling", contemporary construction methods and standardization which were at the core of Aalto's preoccupations at the time and well beyond (re. his often-stated reference to "flexible standardization", to providing housing and other culturally-related solutions for the "little man", etc.).

It seems though that Aalto, "in the only group of artists of which he was a member for a time, the CIAM, [...] appeared from the start as a dissident and observer rather than a comrade-in-arms".[44]

And such was the case at the 4th Congress during the Athens deliberations, which followed its initial part from Marseilles to Piraeus on the Greek steamer *Patris II*. Aalto was not present in spite of Giedion's exhortation, when he wrote to him in advance: "Athens is expecting a lecture from you. Kindly bring not only your genius but also suitable slides. We shall meet in Marseilles on the 27th [July 1933]."

Aalto's "genius", itself being still absent on the 3rd of August, was instead fervently praised by his Swiss mentor and CIAM's Secretary General during his speech in Athens: "Finland in the North is integrally represented by the genius of Aalto, a rare genius in the sense that he responds to the complex problems of our culture [civilisation] away from worn-down prejudices." Albeit *in absentia*, "Der Magus des Nordens" had from the start made his strong presence felt amongst the numerous international and Greek colleagues![45]

In his absence, Aalto had instead sent Nils-Gustav Hahl, not an architect himself, but snobbishly critical when writing to him: "The foredeck [of *Patris II*] is full of yelling Greeks of all sexes and sizes who sleep under the open sky, an inferno [...] and you begin to realize that the ship contains a concentration of specifically Levantine life." In a more composed mood, Hahl went on to inform Aalto on such issues as "maps, photos and descriptions of thirty cities", as well as on his interpretation of what should be labelled the "unfunctional" rather than the "functional city", etc. No other Finnish national was onboard, neither were Gropius, Lurçat, Breuer, Neutra and other known architects, who were missing from the Athens CIAM. Nevertheless, Le Corbusier was the key figure around whom there was always a considerable group of attentive listeners.[46] So was Sigfried Giedion.

---

44. Göran Schildt, *Alvar Aalto, The Early Years*, op. cit., p. 18.

45. S. Giedion, "The Actual state of contemporary architecture", in *Τεχνικά Χρονικά/Technika Chronika/Annales Techniques*, 15 Oct.-15 Novembre 1933, p. 1139. Giedion referred to Aalto as "Der Magus des Norden/The magician of the North" in a postcard sent to him in 1933. The same title has been used in a book edited by Bruno Mawrer and Teppo Jokinen, describing Aalto's relationship with Switzerland (Publisher GTA Verlag, 1998). Information supplied by Tuula Pöyhiä.

46. Göran Schildt, *Alvar Aalto, The Decisive Years*, Otava, Helsinki, pp. 90-102.

39. *Participants of the 4th CIAM in front of the Propylaea at the Acropolis of Athens.*

In a letter –published later as an account of his trip in *Hufvustadsbladet*– Hahl also informed Aalto about a lecture by Le Corbusier, "the renowned father and prophet of Functionalism". This specific mention provides an indication of the approximate date when Aalto had finally reached Athens, between the 4th and the 8th of August 1933 [Hahl might be referring to Le Corbusier's lecture on "Air, son, lumière", given at the Technical Univeristy of Athens in the afternoon of August 3]. One could guess that the night train which Aalto took from Thessaloniki arrived in the early morning in Athens, most probably towards the end of the aforementioned timespan.[47] It was within this same span of 4-5 days that most delegates were absent visiting the Saronic and Aegean islands, and archaeological sites.[48] Be that as it may, Aalto was at least able to listen to Fernand Léger's lecture in the afternoon of August 9th, before the closing reception hosted by the Greek delegation of the CIAM and the rector of the Technical University of Athens. Hahl's reference attests to this fact, as well as to the fact that Aalto had indeed travelled back from Piraeus to Marseilles on board of the *Patris II*, together with the initial participants. He thus mentions later in the *Tulenkantajat* review:

40. *Le Corbusier surrounded by willing listeners on the deck of the steamer* Patris II *(1933).*

47. Eric Mumford mentions only that "Aalto joined the group in Athens for the return voyage". *The CIAM Discourse*, op. cit., p. 78.

48. See i.e. Sigfried Giedion's *CIAM at Sea*, transl. Morton Shand. eds. Jane B. Drew and Trevor Dannatt, *Architects' Yearbook*: 3, pp. 36-39. Also, Matina Kousidi, *Through the Lens of Sigfried Giedion; Exploring Modernism and the Greek Vernacular in Situ*, published in the RIHA Journal 0136, 15-07-2016.

> Fernand Léger gave a lecture on the significance of colours in architecture. This gave rise to an interesting debate, in which Le Corbusier and Alvar Aalto took part enthusiastically.

... and further, while returning on board the *Patris II*:

> At the break of dawn, sleeping in our folding chairs on top deck [...] –we are sometimes awakened by a faint whirring: a few feet of film have turned in Moholy's [Nagy] camera. He gives a sly wink and tiptoes up to the next chair: the camera whirls and the facial movements of the sleeping Alvar Aalto are immortalized.[49]

Aside from pictures of Aalto standing on the deck of *Patris II,* his participation in the return trip was further documented through one of his interventions in German, where he took a position on the debate about the formulation of the Congress "Résolutions". In answering a previous remark made by van Eesteren on not risking "a false resolution", he argued as follows:

> Our Congress cannot escape the obligation of a certain tempo. We can not work endlessly on a problem. Scientific urban planning does not exist, the city is a much too complicated organism. We have to go back to the general topic of this year in detail. [...] Only in this way can we gradually clarify the general problem. The Congress is a meeting point, not a legal body. The resolutions are supposed to be accepted, but at the same time we have to say that this does not end the work of the urban planner, but that one has to go further and further into the individual components in order to make the whole thing more precise.[50]

---

49. in G. Shildt, *Alvar Aalto; The Decisive Years*, op. cit., pp. 90-102.

50. Dated 12 August 1933 / 11 30 'to 13 30' clock. Published in *Τεχνικά Χρονικά/TechnikaChronika/ Annales Techniques*, 15 Oct.-15 November 1933, p. 1180.

41. *Aalto on the deck of* Patris II *from Piraeus to Marseilles (August 1933). Behind him, Otto Neurath and Laszlo Moholy-Nagy.*

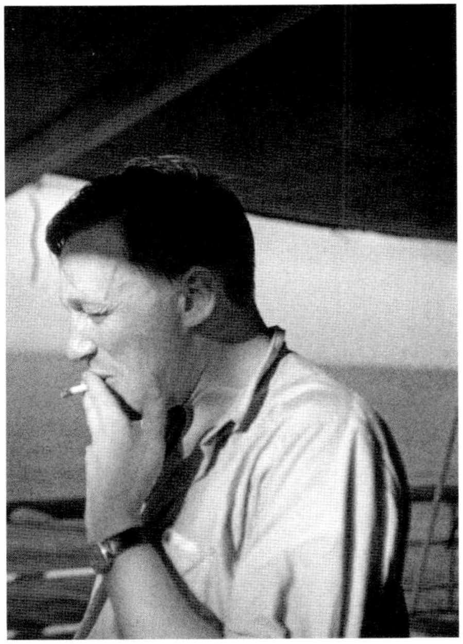

42, 43. *Two close-up photographs of Alvar Aalto on the deck of* Patris II *during its return trip from Piraeus to Marseilles in August of 1933 (© Hazen Sise fonds, Canadian Centre for Architecture, Gift of the Hazen Sise family).*

AALTO AND THE ANTIQUITIES OF ATHENS

ON AND AROUND THE ACROPOLIS

The "beautiful girl" whose one leg was enveloped in white plaster whom Aalto encountered on the night train from Thessaloniki, though arousing his compulsive instinct to charm her, became an allegory – albeit in jest – for the "authentic form" of his "dreams" of Greece; nevertheless, the allegory could not have blurred his vision of what in his cultivated mind represented the epitome of Hellenic culture: the Acropolis of Athens. However, the knowledge which he had acquired of the monument, i.e. from studying Auguste Choisy's drawings or other relevant sources, or even having possibly been informed by his contemporary Hilding Ekelund, was at the time nothing more than a representation; an icon of what he could possibly expect to see. Indeed, the "virtual" could never have matched the "real", even in a mind as imaginative and intuitive as Aalto's, as it didn't in Le Corbusier's either, or for that matter in any other's *a priori* perception or insight, simply acquired from either pictures, *cartes postales*, or drawings.

Witnessing the Acropolis *in situ*, Hahl had already communicated his judgement, thus reinforcing Aalto's inclined interest in being there, browsing the monument with his own eyes and senses, as opposed to a general disfavor of "meetings and museums": "One impression, the first, dominates all others: The Acropolis", stressed Hahl.

In his biographical essays, Göran Shildt later wrote about the "stifling straightjacket" of the Charte d'Athènes and further indicated that Aalto's "confrontation with the unrealistic utopianism and barren theories of the participants of the Athens Congress aroused his instinctive opposition. Instead of taking part in the debates, he sat in the shadow of the Parthenon".

It was precisely on the Acropolis, the city's [*πόλις*] edge point [*άκρον*], that Aalto had chosen to be during the three or so days of his short stay in Athens. There, further comments Schildt, his "ambition to design sterile, differentiated cities in the manner of the Athens Charter vanished and was replaced by the wish to create modern city centers with the same monumental dignity and practical functionality as the Acropolis of Athens once had".[51]

Just before embarking on the return trip to Marseilles, Alvar wrote to Aino:

> What a city this is. Yesterday and today I spent all morning on the Acropolis [...] Sitting on the shady side of temple ruins has proven quite sympathetic after all compared to meetings and museums. I photographed a lot, we will see how they come out.

During his two days' wanderings on the Acropolis and surrounding monuments, Aalto used his camera instead of sketching in any *carnet*, which he anyway did not have on him. Perhaps he had not yet mastered the sketching skills which he demonstrated during his trips from the 1940s onwards, including the one to Greece twenty years later.

In the short time he could spend relating to the magnitude and diversity in scale, form, spatial disposition, and to the history and meaning conveyed by the monuments, Aalto had thus deliberately chosen to use the means of photographic *clichés* which could sustain and revive his mnemonic function for the place he had been and moved around, and for what he had momentarily absorbed. In this way, Aalto was able to convey his sense of visual, tactile and kinetic "space of perception", moving as the ancient Greeks, along the "humble serpentine path leading to the Propylaea",[52] into the cosmos of his "space of memory".

As W. Curtis has put it in a slightly different way: "Aalto was drawn to the classical world, and to the forceful interaction of the intellectual with the sensual in the architecture of ancient Greece."[53]

Furthermore, during his Acropolis experience Aalto witnessed the ancients' means of achieving a scale proper to the human –the *μέτρον άριστον*, referring to either the *individual* or the *collective* [re. the *Agora*]. He could have further noticed the abolition of frontality, the aforementioned winding movement produced by geological and geomorphic particularities, and the composite, *heterotopic* and symbiotic character of a unique cultural and natural landscape; complex, timeless, maturing and ageing through the passing centuries.

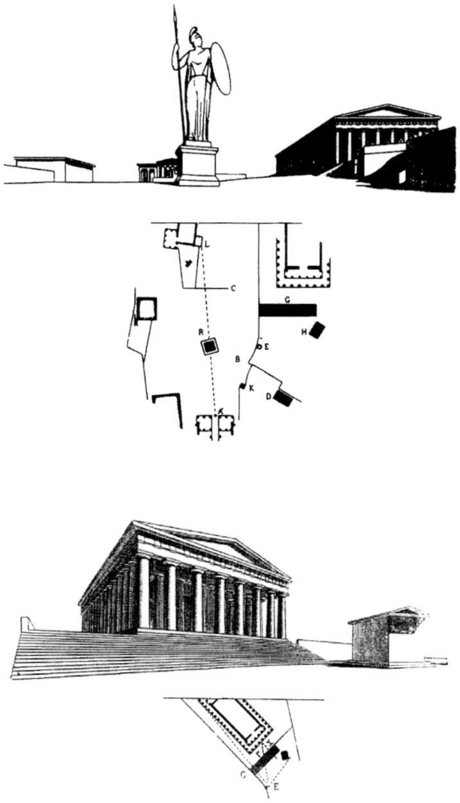

44. *Auguste Choisy's analysis-tracings of the Acropolis monuments.*

51. G. Schildt, op. cit., p. 102.

52. This refers to an observation by the Academician Manolis Korres, the foremost scholar on the archaeology of the Athenian Acropolis and architect of the immense task of the contemporary Acropolis Restoration Project.

53. W. Curtis, op. cit., p. 461.

45. *Three snapshots taken by Aalto from the Acropolis, and a fourth likely taken by someone else of the Odeon of Herodus Atticus with Aalto (?) seated in an upper row (1933) (© Aalto Family/ Alvar Aalto Archives).*

Such experiences might fully justify metaphors attempted by a number of scholars, indicating the possible propinquities between the architect's projects and principles borrowed from the era of Hellenic classicism. Accordingly, the Säynätsalo complex has for instance been compared to a "little Acropolis", or that the Turun Sanomat Building was indicative of the architect's "thorough knowledge of the disposition of columns in Greek temple plans".[54]

In whichever sense such analogies could be pertinent, they would however have to be interpreted with a pinch of salt. Nobody can assess what went on in the cultivated mind of the creative architect, whose strength of structural or inductive intuition lay in the realm of the un- or sub-conscious, relating perhaps more to consecutive iterations of the kind of an *écriture automatique*.[55] One thing is however certain about Aalto's creativity; his capability of accepting "impulses [...] with open eyes".[56]

---

54. Richard Weston, *Alvar Aalto*. London 1995, p. 137, and William Curtis, op. cit., p. 343.

55. Aalto explained his creative process in the following terms: "*I forget the whole maze of problems for a while, as soon as the feel of the assignment and he innumerable demands it involves have sunk into my subconscious. I then move on to a method of working that is very much like abstract art. I simply draw by instinct, not architectural syntheses, but what are sometimes quite childish compositions, and in this way, on an abstract basis, the main idea gradually takes shape, a kind of universal substance that helps me bring the numerous contradictory components into harmony.*" Alvar Aalto, *Sketches*, ed. G. Schildt, tr. Stuart Wrede. Cambridge, Mass.: MIT Press, 1978, p. 97. Also mentioned in K. Jormakka et al., *The Use and Abuse of Paper; Essays on Alvar Aalto*. Tampere Univ. of Technology 1999, p. 30.

56. See "Motifs from past ages" (1922), in Göran Schildt (ed.), *Alvar Aalto in His Own Words*, Otava Publishing Co, Helsinki, 1997, p. 35.

AALTO'S CONTACTS AND THE GREEK DELEGATES AT THE 4th CIAM

46. *Säynätsalo Town Hall - "The little Acropolis" (photos by K. Xanthopoulos. © KX Archive 1978).*

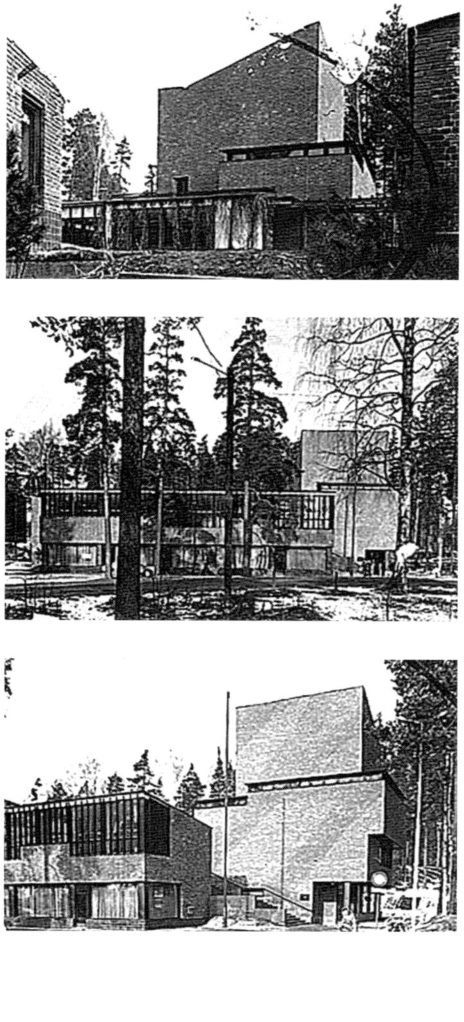

As previously indicated, in 1933 Aalto was already a rising star at the core of the international circle of architecture. He had already met Le Corbusier, Gropius, Giedion, Moholy-Nagy, to name just a few. He had already completed his *tour de force*, the Paimio Sanatorium (1932) with its ingenious elaboration of functionalist principles, and had made it accessible prior to the 4th CIAM through the pages of *Arkkitehti*. His fame had reached the young Greek architects of the time, before he had even shown up in Athens. It is questionable however if and to what extent he had met with his Greek colleagues, participants or outsiders at the Congress, and whether he was aware of their contributions to the modern movement, as a great number of them had already been the object of distinction and praise.

What Kirmo Mikkola had noted about the effects of Functionalism as creating an "unprecedented new optimism [which] imbued the intellectual [re. cultural] life in Europe", did not exclude Greece and that which was taking place in the country during a good part of the 1930s.[57]

In the new, post-1922 Greece, a similar thrust towards the *Functionalist* movement prevailed amongst young Greek architects of the same period, as was by analogy the case in Finland. Added to this, there was an extraordinary, rather explosive, surge of cultural activity encompassing architecture, the visual and applied arts, as well as literature, much of which also expressed the need to assert a new progressive identity

57. Summary by Kirmo Mikkola in *Funkis; Suomi nykyaikaa etsimässä*. Finnish Museum of Architecture, exhibition catalogue, 1980, p. 85 and last page.

with strong social and aesthetic undertones. The movement had a definite impact and resulted in a substantial number of architectural and engineering projects all the way till the end of the 1930s. A few of these projects were the object of encomiums during the CIAM in Athens, by Giedion, Le Corbusier, Moholy-Nagy, Maria Pietro Bardi, and other delegates.[58]

As a corollary to the rationalist ideas connecting Functionalism to the so-called International Style, a back-to-the-roots movement, as well as to the reincarnation of the classical spirit in modernity, was growing in parallel. The regionalist idea of embedding a sense of "Greekness" in architecture and the arts, relating culture to the *topos*, to the environment and climate, was exerting a counter-influence, reiterating in a sense a contemporary analogue of the older *querelle des anciens et des modernes*; the on-going unilateral dichotomy between *art* and *science*, *feeling* and *reason*, adapted to the specific circumstances of space, time and technicity. Aside from the distinction of the former as responding to the *collective* while the latter refers to the *individual*, there were concomitant, related issues distinguishing the two general socio-political and economic ideologies: those of *socialism* and *liberal capitalism*, with their respective technocratic impulses.

In spite of sharp distinctions between the two currents serving more conceptual understandings, the young Greek modernists were also consciously attached to the idea of fusing architectural characteristics, long-established by the vernacular technicians of the Aegean islands and of the mainland, to modernism. As K. Tsiambaos pointed out, "the new generation of Greek architects promoted themselves as both Greek and European, both national and international at the same time".[59] An equivalent degree in Aalto's consecutive steps towards modernity could be assessed as well (re. adaptation of classicism, the Karelian vernacular, etc.), before establishing his own very personal syntactic vocabulary, escaping dogmatic classifications, but at the same time, conveying a sense of "Finnishness".

47. *Building housing the Kitchen and Laundry, Sotiria Hospital Complex (1938). Architect: Periklis Georgakopoulos (1904-1975). An outstanding example of Functionalist architecture towards the end of the 1930s.*

48. *The early "high-tech" train terminal in Piraeus, built from 1926-1929, designed by architect Ioannis Mich. Axelos (1874-1940) and his brother, structural engineer Miltiades Axelos (© ΗΣΑΠ Archives).*

58. See i.e. Pietro Maria Bardi's commendations in "Cronaca di viaggio" published in *Quadrante* 5 of September 1933, translated into Greek by Andreas Giacumacatos as *Ταξίδι στην Ελλάδα· αρχιτεκτονική και πολιτική στην Μεσόγειο του Μεσοπολέμου/Trip to Greece; architecture and politics in the Mediterranean during the inter-war period*, MIET Publ., 2016, pp. 79, 81, 85, 86, 88, 92, 98 and 99.

59. Tsiambaos, Kostas, *An Identity Crisis of Architectural Critique. Architectural Histories*, 2(1), Art. 6, 2014. DOI: http://doi.org/10.5334/ah.bi/ EAHN/ European Architectural History Network.

49. *Among the projects visited by Giedion and other delegates of the 4th CIAM was the Villa Fakidis on the coast at Glyfada, by architect Stamo Papadaki (1932-1933).*

50. *The Kalisperi Primary School in the proximity of the Acropolis by architect Patroklos Karantinos (1931). His school projects were published in* l'Architecture d'Aujourd' hui *(AA) # 4, May 1934 along with Nikolaos Mitsakis', and in* Architettura *3, 1935 (pp. 161-167), as well as in* AA *# 10 of 1938 together with an overview of modern Greek architecture in the 1930s (article by J. Lyghizos, "Mouvement architectural en Grèce", pp. 57-65).*

Who were then some of the young Greek exponents of the modern movement, more or less present at or around the CIAM of 1933, being there during Aalto's presence?

Among those present, most prominent were Ioannis Despotopoulos (1903-1992), Stamo Papadaki (1906-1992), Patroklos Karantinos (1903-1976), and the artist-painter Nikos [Hadjikyriakos] Ghika (1906-1994). Christian Zervos (1889-1970), a Greek *métèque* in Paris, founder of the *Cahiers d'Art* (1926-1960) and close friend of Le Corbusier and later of Aalto, was at the time a member of the French delegation. He was a staunch participant during the whole period of the 4th CIAM right from its start, and instrumental to having the Congress organized on board the *Patris II* and in Athens.

Constantinos Doxiadis (1913-1975), Georgios Candilis (1913-1995) and Aristomenis Provelengios (1914-1999) were still students at the Technical University of Athens. As with the aforementioned architects, they too had gained experience being more or less close to the emblematic figures at the core of the CIAM scene, Alvar Aalto being one, if not the most important, together with Le Corbusier. Both would reappear subsequently in one form or another during the course of their adult lives and careers.

There is very little information attesting to Alvar Aalto's closer relationships with the Greek architects during the 4th CIAM and later; Despotopoulos' contacts and coincidental or pragmatic affinities, and some of Pikionis' parallels in ideological and spiritual beliefs are perhaps the most noteworthy cases of connections to the Finnish master. Given their importance and scope, they are both examined in the separate chapter which follows.

Regarding the other Greek architects, Stamo Papadaki had played a central role both during the cruises back and forth, and in Athens, having been in charge of presenting the plans of Athens. Although Aalto did not get to visit one of his projects, the *Villa Fakidis*, which Giedion, Moholy-Nagy and others had done before, Papadaki was surely known to him, particularly as they travelled together for three days on the way back from Piraeus to Marseilles. Otherwise, there had not been any noticeable contact between the two, apart from a brief message written in French by Papadaki to Aalto. In it, the former expressed the hope that his "cher ami" had retained some nice impressions ("souvenirs") of the country.[60] One could assume that some sort of communication continued to exist between the two men with regard to the CIAM, an issue of common interest.

Thus, for instance, Papadaki, having moved to the U.S. soon after the Athens Congress (1935), sent an invitation to Aalto, who was teaching at M.I.T. at the time, for a meeting to discuss "the next Congress' theme" at the home of Paul Wiener in New York, dated April 10, 1947. (Source of documents: Alvar Aalto Archives, Jyväskylä). As it is known, the CIAM 6 instead took place few months later in Bridgwater, England, in which Aalto did not participate. In the hundreds of letters among the Stamo Papadaki's Papers from 1922-1990,[61] there are no more letters to Aalto, as opposed to a quite substantial correspondence with common friends (i.e. Le Corbusier, Giedion, Moholy-Nagy, Calder, Gropius, and many others).

One could suppose that Aalto had the opportunity to visit Patroklos Karantinos' School adjoining the Acropolis, though this has not been certified or documented, and most probably was not either in his immediate interests. He was anyway well aware of the scale and impact of Karantinos' contribution to modernist Functionalism which were by far more important to him and to its recognition by the Greek and the international architectural community. When observing their contributions to modernity, it may be said that both Stamo Papadaki, Patroklos Karantinos and other Greek modernists then, and indeed later, as i.e. in the cases of Aris Konstantinidis (1913-1993), Dimitris Fatouros (1928-), Dimitris and Suzana Antonakakis (1933- and 1935-), Kyriakos Krokos (1941-1998), and others, were seeking out some common grounds between a modernist simplification and abstraction, and popular roots from the rich vernacular tradition.[62]

Nikos [Hadjikyriakos] Ghika participated in the CIAM deliberations and at least one of the organized excursions to the islands. He was leaning, however, almost exclusively towards the French delegation rather than to the Finnish or others. Ghika had close and friendly relationships with Christian Zervos, Fernand Léger and particularly with Le Corbusier whom he knew from his early years in Paris. At an interview much later, he claimed that his intervention to Le Corbusier was the reason for the 4th CIAM

51. *Photograph taken in 1933 during a trip to Hydra. From left to right: Fernand Léger, Charlotte Perriand, Le Corbusier, Albert Jeanneret, Pierre Jeanneret and Nikos Ghika (not to be confused, as has been the case, with Matila [Costiescu] Ghyka) (© Ghika Gallery Archive, Benaki Museum, Athens).*

60. Letter from Athens dated August 26, 1933. Copy of letter sent to author by Timo Riekko/Alvar Aalto Archives.

61. Stamo Papadaki Papers kept in the Firestone Library of Princeton University -Department of Rare Books and Special Collections, Manuscript Division.

62. See also W. Curtis, op. cit., p. 380, and Alexander Tzonis' reference to "critical regionalism".

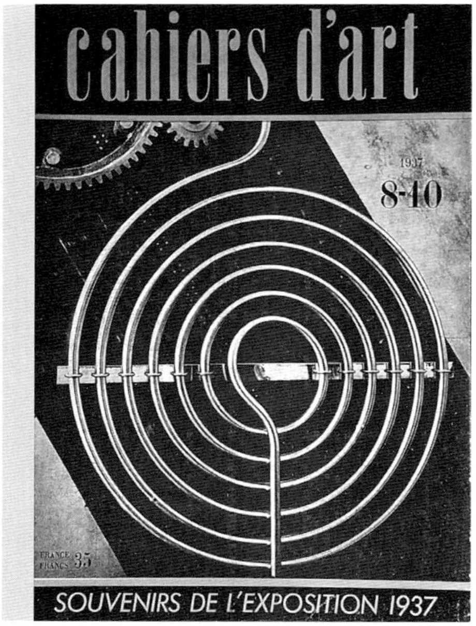

52. *Front cover of the* Cahiers d'Art *8-10 1937.*

53. *Photograph of Aalto's Turun Sanomat building, published in the first issue, of* 20ός Αιώνας/20ème Siècle *in French.*

54. *Photograph of Aalto's Paimio Sanatorium published in the 2nd Greek issue of* 20ός Αιώνας. *The title of the article signed by Alvar Aalto (translated into Greek from German) is: "The Sanatorium of the Finnish architect Aalto (Technical description of the building sent by [the architect] himself from Marseilles)", pp. 31-35.*

taking place in Athens after the Moscow candidacy was turned down following the announcement from the President of the Soviet Tsentroshilsoyuz.[63] Ghika's claim is however questionable, as it has been amply documented that Marcel Breuer and after him Christian Zervos were the instigators of the idea.[64]

A friendship grew between Alvar Aalto and Christian Zervos ever since the Athens Congress. Soon after, Aalto sent Zervos two brochures of his works, the Paimio Sanatorium (referred to by Zervos as "la maison de santé") and the Viipuri Library, for potential publication in the *Cahiers d'Art*. In November 18, 1935, Zervos wrote: "Mon cher Aalto, J'ai reçu les deux brochures [...] Je serais très content de recevoir de bonnes photographies pour les reproduire dans le 1er numéro de la prochaine année."[65]

A similar exchange occurred later when the *Cahiers d'Art* published Aalto's Finnish Pavilion at the Paris International Fair of 1936.[66] In the related text, Aalto was referred to as "occupying nowadays the most eminent place in the movement towards the architectural renovation".

But it was in fact during Aalto's trip to Paris in 1937, that their friendship acquired tighter links. As Göran Schildt points out, Zervos introduced him to "many of the avant-garde artists in Paris, including Constantin Brancusi, with whom he kept in contact for the rest of Brancusi's life". According to an interview related to the two men's mutual esteem, Maire Gullichsen had confirmed it much later, using a statement by Aalto at the time: "Now we'll go and see the Zervos' and Madame Zervos was an utterly wonderful person." It was apparently during the same day at the Zervos' place that she and Aalto were introduced, and also, met Picasso.[67]

If Alvar Aalto received attention and admiration from friends, colleagues and a Greek publisher in France, he had previously ensured for the rise of his reputation among artists and architects in Greece. Already in July 1933, the sculptor Michalis Tombros published the first issue of the magazine *20th Century* [*20ός Αιώνας/20ème Siècle*] in French. Tombros' vision was that the magazine would collaborate with "les noms les plus importants de l'avant-garde internationale". Included in the first issue were, among many other writings and projects, articles by Le Corbusier and Giedion, an essay by Zervos and a photograph of Alvar Aalto's Turun Sanomat building. A few months later (November 1933), in the second edition of *20th Century* in Greek, the

63. Interview of N. Hadjikyriakos-Ghika by the French photographer Jean-François Bonhomme, reproduced in the 5-12-1999 *Το Βήμα/To Vima* newspaper.

64. See i.e. Sibyl Moholy-Nagy, *Experiment in Totality*, Harper & Brothers Publishers, New York 1950, p. 90. Also Andreas Giacumacatos, *Στοιχεία για τη νεότερη Ελληνική αρχιτεκτονική-Πάτροκλος Καραντινός/ Elements about the newer Greek Architecture-Patroklos Karantinos*, MIET Publ., Athens 2003, p. 138.

65. Source of letter: Alvar Aalto Archives, Jyväskylä. Copy sent to author by Timo Riekko.

66. *Cahiers d'Art* 8-10, 1937, pp. 269-270 plus 9 pages of illustrations.

67. G. Schildt, *Alvar Aalto; The Decisive Years*, op. cit., p. 136.

Paimio Sanatorium was presented with a text and pictures sent by Aalto to Tombros as soon as the former had reached Marseilles, or even perhaps from his subsequent short stay with the Giedions in Zurich, in August 1933 [?].[68]

As for Aalto's possible acquaintance with the younger generation of Greek architects, aside from occasional meetings during the CIAM of Athens, there might have been coincidental or random encounters, if at all, mostly at Le Corbusier's cabinet in Paris. Georges Candilis (1913-1995), Aristomenis Provelengios (1914-1999) and Iannis Xenakis (1922-2001) were working there since 1946-1947 after forcefully emigrating together with many others at the start of the Greek Civil War and shortly after [more than one hundred left in December 1945 on board the ship *Mataroa*]. Their arrival signaled the presence of a predominantly left-wing élite, highly distinguished for its contributions to architecture, the arts and letters of France.[69] Aalto would have most probably met Georges Candilis at Le Corbusier's office in Paris. Candilis was at first an active participant in the subsequent CIAMs and later from 1953, a founding member of Team 10. The movement was created as a schism within CIAM, setting a challenge to the latter's doctrinary urbanistic approach. Candilis had also won the international competition for the Free University of Berlin (1963), together with his partners Josic, Woods and Shiedhelm. Aalto must have been very well *au courant* about Candilis' achievements.

68. Also mentioned by A. Giacumacatos, op. cit., pp. 145-146.

69. In addition to the aforementioned, the *Mataroa* passage (December 22, 1945) included a number of architects (Panos Tzelepis, Takis Zenetos, etc.), philosophers (Cornelius Kastoriadis and Kostas Axelos), historians (i.e. Nikos Svoronos), poets and writers (i.e. Mimica Kranaki), artists, educators and scientists. Axelos epitomized the essence of this massive emigration forced by the "White terror"(between 1945 and 1946) at the eve of the Civil War (1946-1949): "Beaucoup d'entre nous sont doublement déçus; déçus par le monde bourgeois dont ils sont issus, rejetant la bourgeoisie, et frustrés par le mouvement communiste. Nous laissions derrière nous la Grèce bourgeoise, nationale et communiste et nous partions à l'étranger dans des pays [France] qui pouvaient nous offrir des opportunités et des possibilités dont plusieurs se sont réalisées." (source: www.info-grece.com/sites/default/.../mataroa-memoire-trouee.pdf). The engineer-architect-composer Iannis Xenakis followed in this deliberate exile two years later, to join soon after Le Corbusier's office.

PIKIONIS' RADICAL PHENOMENOLOGY, DESPOTOPOULOS' SYNTHETIC RATIONALISM, AND ALVAR AALTO

The most influential of all Greeks was Dimitris Pikionis (1887-1968), then Professor at the Technical University. And this, in spite of his low-key presence at the CIAM, as literally an outside spirit standing with his deep critical mind along the fringes of the Congress and its deliberations.

During and after the CIAM, Pikionis considered that the title of "the Organic City" was justified as it related to the problems which the "new architecture" had to confront, both in theory and in practice. In his exhortation on "organicism", he did not solely refer to the physical properties of a place -the topos- but mostly to its "psyche". Concomitantly, he declared the need for the artist/architect to act on two issues:

1. to raise his work up to the rhythm of the site; that is, the harmonization of the dynamics of the spaces, the volumes, the shapes, of the work's material substance, against the dynamics of light, the rhythms of the landscape, the constitution of climate.
2. to subjugate it to the sacred demands of life around it, which presupposes an acute psychological observation and a sensitive heart, as well as the close contact and communication with life and folk.

Furthermore, Pikionis' plea was directed towards serving [local] "culture", rather than importing [foreign] "civilization" and not passively adhering to the dogmas of "contemporary mechanistic prerequisites". "We need", he concluded "to face with a more contemplative manner the solutions offered to us from the West", also urging the selfless youth to exercise the "courage of self-criticism."[70]

It seems that Pikionis did not have at that time or later any personal contacts with Alvar Aalto, neither was he known in Finland, as contrasted to some decades later. His trajectory through modernism, alluded to above, was quite short and ambiguous. Around the end of the 1920s, he had expressed his positive view on it: "When I got to know about this movement [Modernism] I realized that only one step was separating me from it". However, this "step" seemed to elude him, in spite of the sensible rationale established through his modernist oeuvre of 1933, the School at Pefkakia, Lykabettus in Athens; a building complex that remains up to this day a landmark, subjected to consecutive references and analyses, locally and internationally, pretty much as is the case with the Paimio Sanatorium.[71]

Years later, during an interview, he confirmed his "onto-topographical" sensibility and his digression from the rules of modernist rationality, from the "too regular": "I could not admit straight lines, or curves too regular. My paths must follow the jaggedness of the rock."[72]

Around the mid-1930s Pikionis decisively declared: "From that period [1935] there was a change of direction in my aesthetic approach", admitting at the same time that he owed to modern art [incl. architecture] the means for the understanding of tradition (ancient and folk).[73] It is basically from that period that Pikionis' work represented "a dense conversation with time and history to the degree that the design appears as a product of anonymous tradition without drawing attention to the individual creator", as Juhani Pallasmaa had perceptively commented.[74]

55. *School in Pefkakia in the lower western side of the Lykabettus Hill in Athens, by architect Dimitris Pikionis (1933).*

56. *Dimitris Pikionis (1887-1968) (photo by Paul Mylonas. ©Agni Pikioni and Dora Pikioni).*

70. In "Dimitris Pikionis, 'Για ένα Συνέδριο/On a Congress'" in *Κείμενα/ Texts*, op. cit., pp. 168-170.

71. See i.e. Dimitris Antonakakis, *Δημήτρης Πικιώνης· δύο διαλέξεις/ Dimitris Pikionis; two lectures*, Δομές/Domes Publ. Athens 2013. Also, William Curtis, *Modern Architecture since 1900*, London: Phaidon Press, 1996, p. 380.

72. D. Pikionis, in "Virtue and Form", article by David Holden in *The Guardian*, 22 August 1963.

73. Agni Pikioni and Michael Parousis, eds. Δ. Πικιώνης Κείμενα/D. Pikionis Texts, MIET, Athens 1987, p. 33, and Tina Karali, "Μοντερνισμός και Ελληνικότητα στα Cahiers d'Art/Modernism and Greekness in the Cahiers d'Art", in *Ελληνική Αρχιτεκτονική στον 20ό και .../Greek Architecture in the 20th...* op. cit., ed. Andreas Giacumacatos. 2016, p. 117.

74. In Juhani Pallasmaa, *Hapticity and Time; Notes on fragile architecture -"Images of fragile architecture"* (From a text originally delivered for the 1999 RIBA Discourse Lecture).

57, 58. *Pikionis' landscape tracings and the tactile paving of the pathways around the Acropolis (photo by Hélène Binet).*

Furthermore, Pikionis was set to openly deplore any appeal to "casual dogmas and ready-made solutions". Instead, "energy, clearly personal inspiration" were needed, thus allowing [the architect] to overcome the narrow limits of rationalism and standardization.[75]

Pikionis' concept on the *cosmos* of the *organic*, or his "ecological insistence on the interdependency of culture and nature", which according to Kenneth Frampton gives "Pikionis' work a critical edge that is as relevant today as it was thirty years ago", comes very close to Aalto's relative pronouncements, his "forest wisdom" and "synthetic landscape". So does the former's human-centered ideology accounting for the social dimension of modern architecture "as an architecture for people" as compared to Aalto's insistence on an architecture for his "little man".

In addition, Pikionis constantly delved into the "truth" which lies hidden in the primordial use of materials, their technicity and craftsmanship. He believed and admired the wisdom of the "constructional a prioris" identifying Greek vernacular architecture, which he considered "universal and essentially phenomenological". He thus came close to a penchant for Japanese building culture and harmonious order, obvious i.e. in his design of the entrance gate to Filothei's Children's Park, or at the elevated ground floor of the Loumbardiari pavilion and the use of stone footings at the base of its columns. These were qualities inherent as well in Aalto's "sensual feeling for materials" and his critical thinking and work in general. Aalto's *japonisme* in the use of materials and techniques at the Villa Mairea and its winter garden, or even, in the subtle interweaving of architecture with landscape and nature legible at his Muuratsalo Experimental House, project equivalent insights.[76]

A great deal has been written about Dimitri Pikionis, but none on the intricate symbolisms relating him to Alvar Aalto. The divergence in the physiognomy of their creative works could perhaps account for the absence of any critical apposition between the two, albeit one could assert that in many a theoretical and philosophical issue, Pikionis had *in-* and *con-spirito* been "meeting" on common grounds with Aalto, and vise-versa. The only attempt (to the writer's knowledge) that has somehow mended this "flaw" could be attributed to Pallasmaa, in his view of differentiating architecture in relation to memory. He thus writes about a *kind* of architecture as product of a "po-

75. Kostas Tsiambaos' latest treatise, *Αμφίθυμη νεωτερικότητα. 9+1 κείμενα για την μοντέρνα αρχιτεκτονική στην Ελλάδα/Ambivalent Modernism; 9+1 texts about modern Architecture in Greece.* Thessaloniki, Epikentro 2017, pp. 144-145.

76. See: a) Kenneth Frampton in "Dimitris Pikionis 1887-1968", Museum of Finnish Architecture Exhibition Catalogue, 24.11.1993-16.1.1994, p. 70; b) Panayotis Tournikiotis, *The Historiography of Modern Architecture*, Cambridge and London: The MIT Press, 1999, pp. 55-56; and c) Demetri Porphyrios' paper at *The 2nd International Alvar Aalto Symposium*. Publisher: Suomen Arkkitehtiliitto/Suomen rakennustaiteen museo/Alvar Aalto Museo. ed. Asko Salokorpi, Helsinki 1985, pp. 188-203.

etic chemistry", that "creates a sense of deep time, and epic continuity without direct formal reference, as the works of Alvar Aalto, Dimitris Pikionis and Carlo Scarpa".[77]

In July 30, 1965, the Greek architect Ioannis Despotopoulos (alias Jan Despo), *o. Professor an d.TH Athen u. Akademie in München*, sent a letter to Alvar Aalto in German, referring to him as "Sehr geehrter Herr Kollege!" In it he asked Aalto if he "could accept an invitation from TH [the Technical Univerity/Polytechneion] to give a lecture". He further added that "a group of Greek students of the TH in Athens, made a real choice to undertake a pilgrimage [study trip] to Finland", and that as a follow-up, they would "work out a kind of doctoral thesis about your [Aalto's] work in Finland and complete it as a final lecture." Concluding his letter, Despotopoulos underlined that "for the young architects" meeting with him would be "a deep experience".[78]

In the same letter, Despotopoulos introduced himself with a reminder about their past two meetings; the first at the CIAM of Athens and the second in Stockholm together with Ahrbom, which might have occurred during the mid-1950s.[79]

From what is known, Alvar Aalto did not or could not respond to the lecture invitation, at a time when the workload at his office was again at a peak.

Neither did the group of Greek students finally meet with Aalto. What has been documented, though, is that four or five students did indeed travel to Helsinki during the summer of 1965 in order to study and collect material in relation to Aalto's University of Technology main building (design 1953-1955, construction 1964-1966), as well as to other distinguished works on the Otaniemi campus (i.e. Kaija and Heikki Sirén's Chapel). During the spring of 1966, the same students presented their research project at the Athens Technical University with a lecture entitled "Otaniemi".[80]

Although Aalto did not meet for a third time with Despotopoulos, the latter had nevertheless retained his even-tempered esteem for the Finnish master. Accordingly, he

59. *Dimitris Pikionis. Entrance to the Filothei Children's Park (1961-1964).*

60. *Letter by Ioannis Despotopoulos to Alvar Aalto inviting him for a lecture at the TH-Technical University of Athens, sent July 30, 1965 (© Alvar Aalto Archives, Jyväskylä). See also p. 94.*

JAN DESPO
ARKITEKT PROFESSOR

Athen, den 30.7.65.

Herrn
Professor Alvar A a l t o

H e l s i n k i

Sehr geehrter Herr Kollege!

Erstes Mal hatten wir uns beim CIAMcongress in Athen getroffen und letzes in Stockholm beim Kollegen Ahrbom. Wir hoffen Sie in Athen, eventuell bei der Technischen Hochschule zu sehen. Bei dieser Gelegenheit möchte ich fragen ob Sie eine Einladung der TH einen Vortrag zu halten annehmen könnten.
Nun, eine Gruppe griechischer Studenten der TH in Athen, unternehmen eine wahre Wahlfart zu Ihnen nach Finnland.
Anschliessend, werden sie über Ihr Schaffen in Finnland eine Art Doktorarbeit ausarbeiten und als Abschlussvortrag ergänzen.
Für die jungen Architekten wird ein tiefes Erlebnis sein Sie in Finnland treffen zu dürfen.

Mit herzlichen Grüssen

(I.Despotópoulos)
o.Professor an d.TH Athen u.
Akademie in München.

Athen 138 - Mimnermou 2

77. See Juhani Pallasmaa, *Space, Place, Memory and Imagination: The Temporal Dimension of Existential Space – "Architectural amnesia"*, 2007, p. 197.

78. Copy of letter from the Alvar Aalto Archives in Jyväskylä sent to author by Timo Riekko, reproduced here and on p. 94.

79. Nils Ahrbom (1905-1997), the Swedish architect and writer, was a common friend to both Alvar Aalto and Jan Despo. Aalto knew him already since the Stockholm Exhibition of 1930, where Ahrbom had exhibited with Markelius and others, proposals for housing alternatives. It is also known that Ahrbom supported Alvar Aalto's vision of building diversity and standardized building blocks at the Nordic Building Days held in Helsinki in June 1955.

80. According to information provided by Professor Panayotis Tournikiotis, four students traveled to Helsinki in 1965 to carry out research for the lecture they were to give during the spring of 1966, as part of their graduation tasks. They were Maria Drakopoulou, Tasos Emmanouil, Georgios Katevas and Agni Panagiotatou. Before this, the works and thoughts of Alvar Aalto had however been a matter of study and research by other graduating students, when in 1960, Ioanna Pavlaki and Lydia Tazedaki presented a lecture at the Athens Technical University on "The Finnish architect Alvar Aalto".

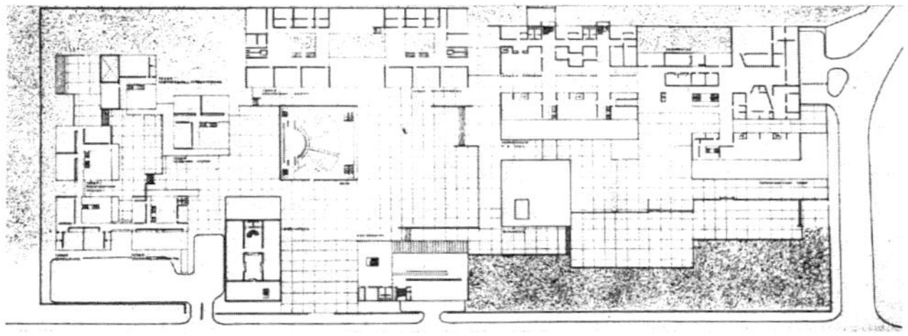

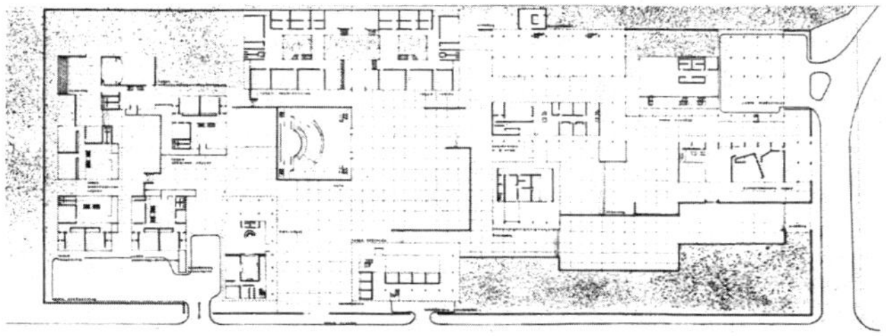

61, 62. *Diploma project, Technical University of Athens, 1965: University complex for a School of Architecture, Urban Planning and Applied Arts, with common student facilities (i.e. Aula in the center facing the main "piazza"). Both Aalto and Despotopoulos occupied the students' minds in their Diploma work submission. Grad. students: K. Xanthopoulos, L. Philippidou and A. Tricha. Professor: Ioannis Despotopoulos. (© K. Xanthopoulos/KX Archive, 1965).*

conveyed to the students aspects similar to Aalto's humanistic and social visions, as exemplified by his dogma-free work, his empirical experience of space and objects, and his intuition for an architecture that would likewise take "a deeper role as a humanizing cultural factor".

Aside from some incidental familiarity that a few Greek architects had about Aalto and his work up to 1960 -Karl Fleig's first AA edition was only published in 1963- it was Despotopoulos who had opened wide the "Aalto Chapter" in Greece, following his return from Sweden and his second nomination as Professor at the TU of Athens in 1961.

The unconventional *teacher* [*δάσκαλος* as his students referred to him] was markedly influenced both by what he had experienced during his studies at the Bauhaus (Weimar 1924-1925) and the TH in Hannover, and also during his initial architectural training at Eric Mendelsohn's office. But equally, if not more important, were his 14 decisive years of practice in Sweden (from 1947-1960). Having been subjected to such rich experience, Jan Despo remained by and large "loyal to the syntactic austerity of the central-European movements of Modernism", as opposed to Alvar Aalto's intuitive design maneuverability.[81]

As it is difficult, if possible at all, to categorize both architects in terms of various stylistic *-isms*, there are rather sound analogies that could bring them close; closer even perhaps than the two meetings which had occurred rather by coincidence in the past. Such analogies could connect to either context or inference, distilled through dictums, writings and projects falling into approximately the same time periods.

Concerning the 1933 CIAM's central theme referring to "the Functional City", Despotopoulos had also adopted instead the terms, "the Organic City" and "contemporary [instead of functional] architecture" (*Neuzeitliche Architektur*), in full conscience of their deeper meaning. In this, he had conceded with Fred Forbat's thesis that the mistakes observed in the urban settlements of the last decades were also due to the neglect of the notion that the city is an organism (*Organismus*) and that life in it depends on the uninhibited and coordinated function of all of its constituent parts (organs). Both stressed that the

81. Panayotis Tsakopoulos, 'The Enigmatic Absence of Ioannis Despotopoulos', in *Reflections on Greek Postwar Architecture*, Kaleidoscope Publ., Athens 2014, p. 133.
See also Telemachos Andrianopoulos, "Luleå-Hudiksval-Αθήνα. Κύκλος-τετράγωνο-κύκλος: τρία θέατρα του Ιωάννη Δεσποτόπουλου/Luleå-Hudiksval-Athens; circle-square-circle: three theaters of Ioannis Despotopoulos", in *Ελληνική Αρχιτεκτονική στον 20ό ... /The Greek City in the 20th ...* op. cit., ed. Andreas Giacumacatos, 2016.

external form of the city is a function (*Funktion*) of the life manifestations included in it, and that its shape could not be the result of purely mechanical considerations.[82]

With respect to the *Chart of Athens*, Jan Despo suggested that "this Chart had to be revised after WWII, as it was of a static content, only good for a 'one-off planning', instrumental of the former non-functional, rather decorative 'non-city'". In a sense, all this brought him close to Hahl and Aalto's remarks made during the trip on board the *Patris II*.[83]

During the CIAM Congress in Sigtuna-Stockholm, Jan Despo as a member of the Swedish team, had composed and presented a so-called *Chart of Athens II*, vested with such dialectical flexibility that it would respond both as a research and synthetic basis to every socio-political and cultural development. However, Despo's initiative did not have any further practical effect, other than adding to the abundant wealth of theoretical stances offered by the CIAMs.

In 1932, Despotopoulos won the architectural competition for the main sanatorium building in Athens, identified as the *Mega Laiko* or *Sotiria Sanatorium*. Hypothetical influences from Aalto's Paimio Sanatorium (1928-1932) have been suggested, but they remain highly questionable. Could Despotopoulos have been acquainted with Paimio already in 1932 or with the competition entries submitted in 1929? The question poses the issue of timing in regards to the first full publication of Aalto's sanatorium in *Arkkitehti*,[84] when Despotopoulos had already completed his design proposal

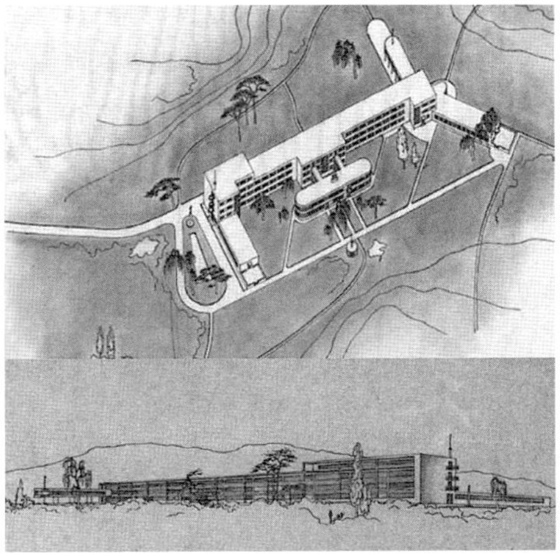

63. *Isometric plan and perspective view of the Sotiria Sanatorium by I. Despotopoulos (© I. Despotopoulos Archives/Archives of Modern Greek Architecture/Benaki Museum, Athens).*

64. *Bird's eye view of Alvar Aalto's Paimio Sanatorium.*

82. See Lina Dima, "Η 'Οργανική Πόλις' του 4ου CIAM και ο Ιωάννης Δεσποτοπουλος/The 'Organic City' of the 4th CIAM and Ioannis Despotopoulos", in *Ελληνική Αρχιτεκτονική στον 20ό ... /The Greek City in the 20th* ... op. cit., ed. Andreas Giacumacatos, 2016, pp. 76-77.

83. L. Dima, op. cit.

84. Drawings and details of Aalto's Sanatorium were published in *Arkkitehti* XXX/1933, in a rather comprehensive way (*Paimion Parantola*, pp. 79-90).
Prior to this, *Arkkitehti* 3/1929 published the competition results with very few representative drawings of four winning proposals (*Varsinais-Suomen Tuberkuloosiparantolan kilpailu*, pp. 42-46), including: 1st Prize *Piirretty Ikkuna* by Alvar Aalto (p. 43); 2nd Prize *Valo* by K. Borg, O. Flodin and Paavo Hanstén (p. 44); 3rd Prize *Ammon-Ra* by Antero Pernaja and Ragnar Ypyä (p. 45); and distinction/acquisition of *Ympyrään piirretty kolmioristi* by Erik Bryggman (p. 46).
First publication of the Paimio Sanatorium (*Sanatorium I Paimio, Finland*) in a foreign (non-Finnish) architectural magazine was in the Swedish *Byggmästaren*, 14/1932 (Arkitektupplagan 5/Architectural supplement 5, pp. 80-83), undersigned by Alvar Aalto.
In a recent paper presented in Rovaniemi, Sotirios Zaroulas, a Greek architect and scholar at the Polytechnic of Milan, made an extensive overview and typological comparison of the 420-bed Sotiria Sanatorium (35,000 sq. m.) of Despotopoulos to the 184-bed Paimio Sanatorium (26,550 sq. m.) of Aalto. See Sotirios Zaroulas, "Paimio as a Model", in *Aalto beyond Finland. Architecture and Design*, Silvia Micheli and Esa Laaksonen, eds., Helsinki: Alvar Aalto Foundation, 2015, pp. 333-339.
In his end remarks he states that: "Despotopoulos discovered the ideal hospital sanatorium in the architecture of Aalto" True as this might be, his further remark that his "hospital model [re Sotiria Sanatorium]" was "inspired by Alvar Aalto's Sanatorium", is indeed questionable, at least during the former's initial design phases. Zaroulas actually writes in the beginning of his paper: "It's not been known yet

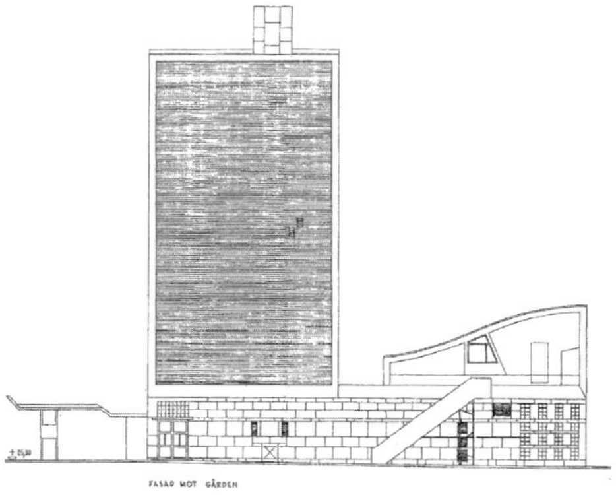

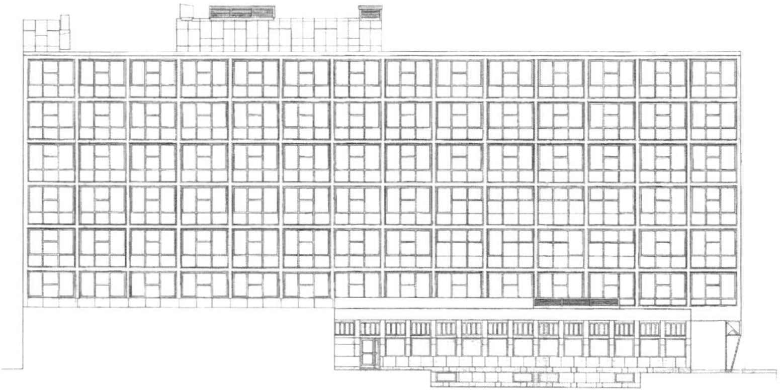

65, 66, 67. *Ludvika, Folketshus, highest wing by Jan Despo (photo 1961). Front and side elevations (supplied by Ulf Johansson, Municipal archivist, Ludvika municipality).*

almost one year earlier. Besides, given the detailed chronology mentioned in Marianna Heikinheimo's doctoral thesis (2016), drawings were supplied by Aalto up till 1932. One should also bear in mind that the two men had met for the first time only in 1933 and publications on Paimio in Greece came after the closing of the 4th CIAM. Therefore alleged "influences" remain questionable. *Sotiria Sanatorium* with its separate physiognomy retains its own distinctive value as an architectural achievement, in a way relatively comparable to Paimio's. Accordingly, it is not surprising that the Report of the Finnish National Board of Antiquities, had selected it in a brief presentation with other four distinguished European sanatorium projects from the 1920s and 1930s.[85]

Jan Despo's experience in Sweden was to a certain degree the most experimental and productive period during his lifetime. Already from the start of his stay there, he found himself at "another home" in which his integration into the social, political [re *the 3rd way to socialism*] and architectural climate was remarkably almost total.

He adopted principles and took active part in institutions such as the Swedish social centers, people's homes (*folketshuset/medborgarhuset*), service homes (*serviceboende*) and health care centers (*hälsovård*). There he found the fertile ground on which he could apply his ideological and architectonic beliefs, the role of his *agora* and open theater concepts, much in an improvised line to his mentor's Walter Gropius. Out of the many social and community center projects he had designed, i.e in Luleå, Östersund,

---

how Despotopoulos became acquainted with the architecture of Aalto's sanatorium."
A similar hypothesis has been presented by Panayotis Tsakopoulos in a footnote in his book. He writes: "We should consider certain that Despotopoulos knows Aalto's pre-war work, particularly the Paimio Sanatorium (1928/29-1933), whose synthesis seems to have influenced the design of the Sotiria Sanatorium (1931-43)" (P. Tsakopoulos, op. cit., footnote 29, p. 422).

85. National Board of Antiquities, Nomination of Paimio Hospital for inclusion in the *World Heritage List*, Helsinki 2005. Authors: Margaretha Ehrström, Sirkkaliisa Jetsonen, Tommi Lindh, Monica Schalin, Mona Schalin, p. 41.

Hudiksvall, etc., the only one built was the *Folketshus* for the Ludvika kommun (design commission 1949, built 1955-1957).[86] At that time Jan Despo was well aware of Alvar Aalto's work and had most likely been impressed by his earlier Town Center proposal designed in 1944 with Swedish architect Albin Stark for the Community of Avesta (This design proposal, which never came into being, had very little, if anything, to do with another building complex designed 15 years later on a different site, known as Avesta's *Aalto Huset* or *Sundh Center*, after the name of its builder and original owner).

In 1963, Jan Despo provided a condensed version of his Swedish experience and his crystalized ideas on the cultural content and identity of *Social Centers* and the *Agora* in his article "Das neuzeitliche Kulturzentrum-die Agora", published in the German review *Bauen+Wohnen* (17:2, pp. 49-61). There, he "meets" Alvar Aalto again whose *Wolfsburg Cultural Center* was also published in the same issue (pp. 63-72) with an introduction by Jürgen Joedicke.

As if by a sheer paradox of Socratic irony, these parallel publications acted as preambles to two of the architects' most important visionary projects: Aalto's proposal for the new Center of Helsinki (approved in 1961 and 1966), and Despotopoulos' proposal for the new Cultural Center of Athens (competition 1959, design from 1960-1962 and 2nd proposal 1968-1973).

Both proposals incorporated on a grand scale many of the ideological values thought about and voiced on several occasions by the two architect-masters, summed up in the democratic role which a modern city-scape should symbolize, demonstrate and provide for its citizens.

In its edition of February 22nd, 1961, the Swedish newspaper *Svenska Dagbladet* went further by presenting Jan Despo's proposal with the far-sighted title: "Aten kan bli Europeiskt kulturcentrum", thus vesting it with an influence well beyond the boundaries of Athens and Greece.[87]

Jan Despo Alvar Aalto

68. *Photos of Jan Despo and Alvar Aalto printed side-by-side with biographical notes in the initial section of the review* Bauen+Wohnen *(1963).*

86. See Ludvika kommun - Nu finns en trailer för den av kommunen... *https://www.facebook.com/.../videos/1099936523407448/*: "Snart helg, det firar vi med ett par "höjdarbilder" på åtta våningar höga Ludvika Folkets hus, byggt 1955-57 efter att arkitekten Ioannis Despotopoulos (även känd som Jan Despo) hade fått uppdraget 1949. Han var född i Grekland 1903 och avled där 1992, men bodde och var verksam som arkitekt i Sverige under perioden."
On Jan Despo's Swedish experience and work, Panayotis Tsakopoulos has made extensive research both in the Archives of Arkitektur Museet in Stockholm and in the Despotopoulos drawings and documents in the Archives of Contemporary Greek Architecture-Benaki Museum in Athens. See P. Tsakopoulos, "Ioannis Despotopoulos; The Architecture as Manifesto", in *Reflections on Greek Postwar Architecture*, op. cit., pp. 387-427.
It is worth mentioning that Despotopoulos was the only Greek architect who had maintained personal contacts with Giedion, Forbat (when in Sweden), and with the CIAM after WWII, with the exception of Georges Kandilis. See A. Giacumacatos, *Elements about the newer Greek Architecture-Patroklos Karantinos*, op. cit., p. 398.

87. The February 22nd, 1961 article published by *Svenska Dagbladet* (p. 10 A) described in general terms Jan Despo's proposal for the Athens Cultural Centre. The article came as a result of an interview given by Despotopoulos to a journalist undersigned CAL at the architect's "beautiful residence in Bagar-

69, 70. *Alvar Aalto's proposal for the Helsinki City Center (top) and Finlandia talo (photo by K. Xanthopoulos. © KX Archive, 1981).*

71, 72. *Ioannis Despotopoulos' proposal for the Athens Cultural Center (top) and the Athens Conservatory (photo by Georges Fakaros).*

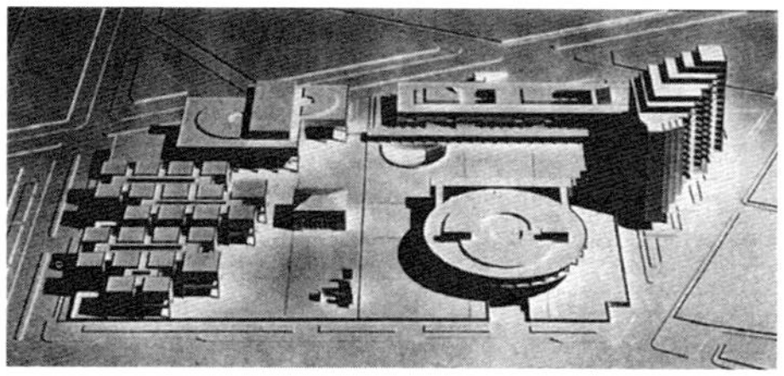

However, both his and Aalto's inspired propositions were instead criticised for their monumentality, being far from people's real needs [?] and habitual civic perceptions, at a time vulnerable to the upcoming wave of massive social unrest. The cultural revolusion of the 1960s was anyway a decade of subversion os established conventions, social and architectural.

Thus, neither the linear deployment of Aalto's visionary project, nor the concentric articulation of the Despotopoulos' were finally realized save one building in each case: the House of Finland (*Finlandia talo*) and the Conservatory of Athens. Their presence, though serving their exclusive purpose and being in themselves prototypes of modernist idioms, remain however enigmatic. As was astutely pointed out, they reveal "the big distance which separates an 'ideogram' from a built work".[88]

From that period onwards Aalto and Despotopoulos both chose a rather discretionary and monastic withdrawal from the main scene. They carried on their important work in a more introverted and meditative mood: *quo vadis architettura*?

mossen in Stockholm". The main title of the article in English was "Athens can become the European Cultural Center", followed by a sub-title identifying the Greek architect as a "Swedish carrier moving a museum so as to resolve the architect's problem". The Swedish identity was rather odd, though understandable in view of the many years the architect had spent and worked in Sweden. The "moving of a museum" obviously made reference to Despotopoulos' proposal to relocate the existing eclectic building of the Byzantine Museum to an adjoining site, so that all other elements could be accommodated as parts of what he deemed a synthetic ensemble.

88. In Dimitris Philippidis, *Νεοελληνική Αρχιτεκτονική/Contemporary Greek Architecture*, Athens, Melissa Publ., 1984, p. 342.

1953. ALVAR AALTO BACK TO GREECE

Avoir choisi Delphes pour y mettre la Pythie est un coup de génie. C'est un paysage à terreurs religieuses, vallée étroite entre deux montagnes presque à pic, le fond plein d'oliviers noirs, les montagnes rouges et vertes, le tout garni de précipices, avec la mer au fond et un horizon de montagnes couvertes de neige.

Gustave Flaubert, 10 Février 1851[89]

In contrast to Aalto's orientations and ambitions during his first short trip to Greece, his second trip twenty years later was a rather deliberate decision involving an esoteric call, something perhaps relating to a quest for a sort of Delphic Oracle. One which could possibly answer his restless sentimental and intellectual impulse at the age of maturity, introspection and recollection. It was a trip which could have enhanced the architect's cultural and architectural horizon and his deeper comprehension of purist *Classicism*, its meaning and proportional value and beauty. Compared to his previous "snapshot" visit to Athens, a hasty escape from duties imposed by the CIAM, this second trip was rather acting as a reminder of a "duty" to himself. He might have wished to acquire an embodied assimilation of the ancient vestiges blending with nature, along the footprints of timeless ruins. Those timeless Greek ruins came as a natural concomitant to others which he had experienced during a trip to Italy and *Magna Grecia* one year earlier (1952).[90]

73. *Serifos. Vernacular architecture as photographed by Göran Schildt during his sailing trips across the Aegean (© The Christine and Göran Schildt Foundation).*

89. "Lettre V" by Gustave Flaubert to Louis Bouilhet, in *Lettres de Grèce*, Éditions du Péplos, 1948.
90. On the subject of ruins, see John Roberts, *Aalto Landscape Ruins*. Alvar Aalto Researchers' Network Seminar – *Why Aalto?* 9-10 June 2017, Jyväskylä.

74. *Delphi. Sketch by Jean-Jacques Baruël. The Athens Treasury on the left and the Temple of Apollo in front of the Theater at the center-right (1951).*

At that time, a further boost to this interest in expanding his trip to Greece might have been his acquaintance in 1952 with his later close friend and main biographer Göran Schildt who had started his many sailing trips to Greece aboard the *Daphne* already since 1950.[91]

It is also known that Jean-Jacques Baruël, then working in Aalto's office, had travelled to Greece during 1951. His information and sketches of Delphi and other places could have triggered the attention of his master and later collaborator (re. Aalborg-NJ Kunstmuseum).[92] Baruël's influence might have been more pronounced with reference to an alleged meeting between Aalto and the then director of the École Française d'Athènes (1950-1969), the archaeologist and proficient scholar on Delphi, Georges

91. Recorded in Göran Schildt's book *I Odysseus' kölvatten*, published by Söderström in 1951, as well as in his books *Daphne och Apollon* (Söderström, 1952), *Purjehdukseni Daphnela* (Otava 1987), etc.
In 2012, the first book was translated and published by Alphatrust in Greek with an introduction by his Greek friend, architect Anthony C. Antoniades. Antoniades was also an invited lecturer on the occasion of a Seminar entitled "The Seven Lives of Göran Schildt" held at the Athens Embassy of Finland in 2014. The title of his lecture was: "Göran Schildt: of the Diaspora, exponentially!", and is part of his extended personal archives, including many messages and letters that were exchanged between the two from early 1980 until Schildt's death in 2009.
Schildt's first trip started in 1950 from Lavagna Italy and included visits to the Greek temple of Paestum/Alikarnassos, Kefalonia, Ithaka, Patras (Gastouni, Olympia), Galaxidi, Itea, Delphi, Corinth (Acrocorinth), Mycenae, Epidaurus, Aegina, Athens (Kaisariani, Acropolis), Sounion, Cythnos, Serifos, Tinos, Mykonos, Delos, Naxos, Ios, Santorini and Heraklion (Knossos). He returned back to Italy sailing from south Peloponnessos. His house on Leros island came much later.

92. On J-J Baruël, see Jaime J. Ferrer Forés, "Alvar Aalto and Jean-Jacques Baruël", *Working papers-Alvar Aalto Researchers' Network*, March 12-14, 2012, Seinäjoki and Juväskylä. Publisher Alvar Aalto Museum.

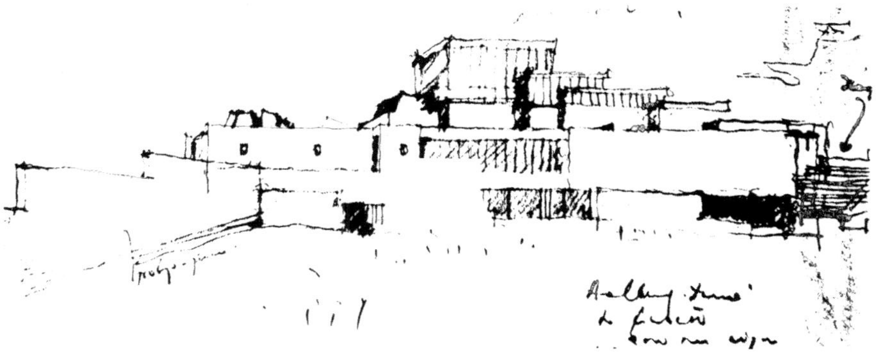

75. *Sketch of Aalborg's Nordjulland Kunstmuseum (sketch by K. Xanthopoulos. © KX Archive, 1978).*

Daux. In a *mémoire* published 12 years after Aalto's death in the Danish architectural review *Arkitekten*, Baruël recollected the following event:

> One day I was called at Alvar's drawing room by Frenchman Georges Daux. [...] I had visited him in Athens, he was the director of the École Française there. At the time I was carrying with me a letter of Edvard Thomsen, then director of the [Danish] Academy of Arts. [...] And now he [Daux] was here in Helsinki with his wife. [...] Daux and Alvar soon became good friends [?]. When Elissa and Alvar got married, I was able to send a telegram to Daux, indicating that they were coming to Athens. Alvar considered that Daux and the École Française were "the place" [to visit] in Athens.[93]

Be that as it may, Aalto's "friendship" with Daux and his exclamation for visiting "the place" are still lacking adequate proof. None of these two conditions to which Baruël alluded to have as yet been found in any archival document, at least in Daux's extensive correspondence record between 1950 and 1955.[94] It is however rather plausible that, either in Helsinki or in Athens, Daux advised Aalto for at least two of the ancient sites for which his expertise was and still remains irrefutable: the sanctuaries of Delphi and of Delos.

93. Excerpt from an article by Jean-Jacques Baruël, "Vennen Alvar Aalto, nogle rids" in *Arkitekten* 4-1988, p. 73.

94. In December 12, 2018, the author searched through all of Georges Daux's correspondence with the assistance of the archivist of the École Française d'Athènes, Marie Stahl, namely: the Série correspondance directoriale/dossier 175 from 1950-1955, the Fonds Georges Daux/FGD from 1951-1954, and the Lettres des directeurs (Georges Daux) from 1951-1954. Further research comprised the site www.calames.abes.fr, without any specific result as to the contacts between Georges Daux and Alvar Aalto, or Georges Daux and Jean-Jacques Baruël.

Furthermore, there are only scarce indications as to when and how Aalto made his second trip to Greece.

In 2006, the National Pensions Institute in Helsinki (1948-1956), published a 50-year commemorative report, in which Timo Tuomi had praised the emblematic building attributing to it characteristics reminiscent of Italian and Greek villages and/or temple sites:

> The different parts of the building are gradually descending into the park zone bringing in mind the Italian or Greek villages or temple sites built on top of the hill, where public space has been lifted to the hill.[95]

The same report revealed an application made by Professor Aalto to the Board of the Bank of Finland for financing "*research assignments* (sic)" to a number of countries including Greece, with the aim of drawing inspiration and useful observations in the course of the project's design conception and qualitative development. In it he asked for the approval of the necessary foreign currency. The application which was submitted by Aalto in April 1953, stated among other things:

> Architect Elsa Mäkiniemi-Aalto [Elissa] and the undersigned [Alvar Aalto] are travelling to Switzerland, Northern Italy, Greece and Denmark for research assignments in connection to the work of the Architectural Office Alvar Aalto. The journey which begins on the 17th of this month involves both architectural research (in Greece Delphi, Mykonos and Epidauros) particularly for the architectural details for the main building of the National Pensions Institute and research on the practical and financial solutions of industrial and office buildings in Switzerland and Northern Italy... With reference to the above, the undersigned hopes that the Board of the Bank of Finland will agree to the submitted currency application.[96]

Elsewhere, from Aalto's office account book dated 17th of April 1953, there was a handwritten entry for the acquisition of one visa to Greece (*Kreikan viisumi*). On the same page one day earlier, there was also an entry for acquiring more than one visa to Italy (*Italian viisumit*).[97]

Does this token of information imply that Alvar Aalto travelled to Greece alone, while he was previously touring with Elissa around Denmark, Switzerland or Italy?

---

95. See: Alvar Aalto, *Ylevöittää Arjen; Kansaneläkelaitoksen päätoimitalo 50 vuoden iässä*. Text: ErkkiSarkkinen. Publ. Kansaneläkelaitos, Helsinki, 2006. http://www.kela.fi/documents/10180/12149/kela_50v.pdf. pp. 18-19.

96. op. cit., p. 19.

97. Page copy from account book supplied to the author by Timo Riekko / Alvar Aalto Archives, Jyväskylä.

Whereas one could be justified in assuming that such was the case, a handwritten letter in two parts addressed by Elissa Aalto to an architect working at the Munkkiniemi office on the Muuratsalo experimental house, defeats this hypothesis. Elissa first started writing the letter in Zurich on April 21, 1953. In it she provides evidence that she and Alvar had flown to the Swiss city from Copenhagen. Most significant, however, was the second part of the letter, which she wrote from Delphi on the 27th of April, where she was indeed visiting the sanctuary alongside Alvar Aalto. It therefore becomes clear that they had both landed in Athens a couple of days or so earlier.[98]

The question arising here has to do with the couple's whereabouts between the 21st and the 25th of April 1953. Where did they come to Athens from?

The Aaltos' traces can in fact be roughly estimated through a number of telegrams sent by their secretary in Helsinki, attesting to the approximate dates of their stopovers and sojourns. The first telegram, dated Friday, April 24th, was sent to the Quirinale Hotel in Rome. Would this mean that the couple flew from Zurich to the *City on seven hills* for a rather short stay before traveling to Athens? However, in her letter Elissa paradoxically mentioned that they had flown to Athens from Zurich and not from Rome! Could it be that after a brief visit to Rome between the 22nd and 25th of April, they returned to Zurich just before travelling to Greece?[99]

A second telegram was sent to the King George Hotel of Athens on Monday, May 4, indicating that Alvar and Elissa had spent nearly 10 days in Greece. The telegram to Athens was informing Alvar Aalto about the exhibition in Vienna of the entries to the architectural competition for a sports, concert, congress and exhibition complex in Vogelkweidplatz, from April 29 to May 9. As is known, Aalto had won First Prize, although the commission to design and build it was instead awarded to the Austrian architect Roland Rainer.

A question remains as to whether the Aaltos had, if at all, visited the Exhibition in Vienna and if so, wherefrom and when. Was it during a brief transit before they flew from Athens to Paris (re. telegram sent to the Hotel De Crillon in Paris on Monday, May 11), or even after, while on their way back to Helsinki placed around Thursday, May 14?

Answers to these questions can still only remain as mere deductions.

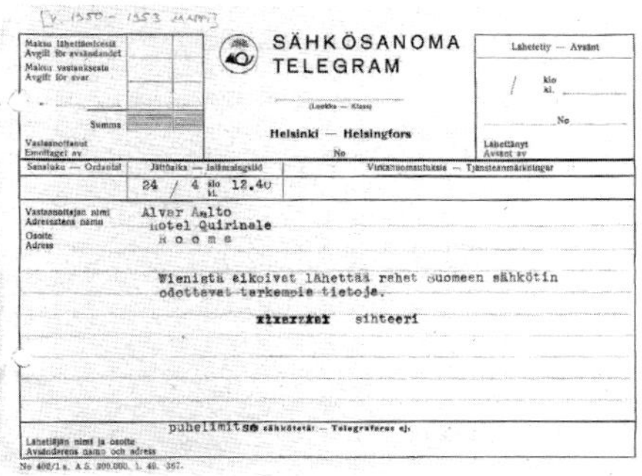
SÄHKÖSANOMA TELEGRAM
Helsinki — Helsingfors
24 / 4 klo 12.40
Alvar Aalto
hotel Quirinale
Rooma
Wienistä aikoivat lähettää rahat suomeen sähkötin odottavat tarkempia tietoja.
sihteeri

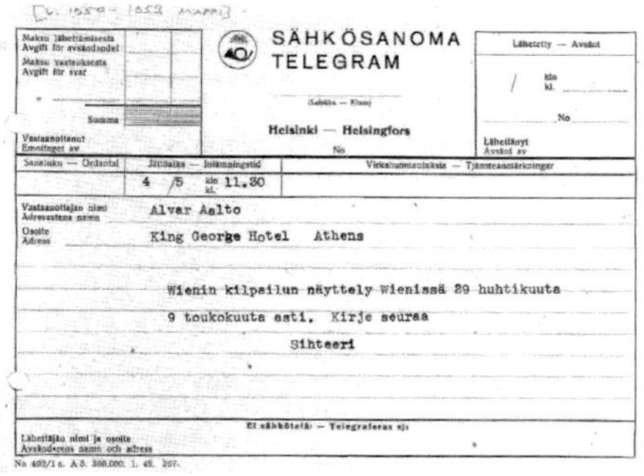
SÄHKÖSANOMA TELEGRAM
Helsinki — Helsingfors
4 /5 klo 11.30
Alvar Aalto
King George Hotel Athens
Wienin kilpailun näyttely Wienissä 29 huhtikuuta
9 toukokuuta asti. Kirje seuraa
Sihteeri

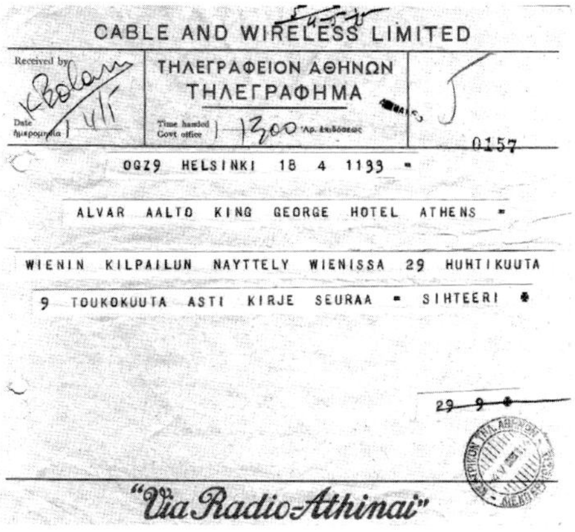
CABLE AND WIRELESS LIMITED
ΤΗΛΕΓΡΑΦΕΙΟΝ ΑΘΗΝΩΝ
ΤΗΛΕΓΡΑΦΗΜΑ
0029 HELSINKI 18 4 1133
ALVAR AALTO KING GEORGE HOTEL ATHENS
WIENIN KILPAILUN NAYTTELY WIENISSA 29 HUHTIKUUTA
9 TOUKOKUUTA ASTI KIRJE SEURAA SIHTEERI
"Via Radio-Athinai"

76, 77, 78. *Telegrams sent to Alvar Aalto in Rome (April 24, 1953) and Athens (May 4, 1953) by his secretary (© Alvar Aalto Archives, Jyväskylä).*

98. Copy of letter handwritten in two phases by Elissa Aalto, from Zurich and Delphi. Alvar's impulsion to sketching "greek walls" "... [with] a drawing pad under his arm..." was noted by Elissa in the 2nd part of the letter: "Alvar painui jo piirustuslehtiö kainalossa piirtämään kreikkalaisia muureja." Document supplied by Timo Riekko / Alvar Aalto Archives, Jyväskylä.

99. Telegram copies supplied to the author in Dec. 12 2018 by Timo Riekko / Alvar Aalto Archives, Jyväskylä. The first was sent by Aalto's secretary to the Hotel Quirinale in Rome (24/4/1953) and referred to the payment of the Prize won at the Architectural Competition for the Sports Hall in Vienna. The second was sent to the King George Hotel of Athens in Syntagma Square (4/5/1953) referring to the above Competition's exhibition dates in Vienna. The third was sent to the Hotel De Crillon in Paris (11/5/1953) with a reminder of a meeting arranged in Helsinki with Eric Blomstedt for Sunday, May 17. In it there was also a question as to Aalto's time of arrival in Helsinki on Thursday, May 14.

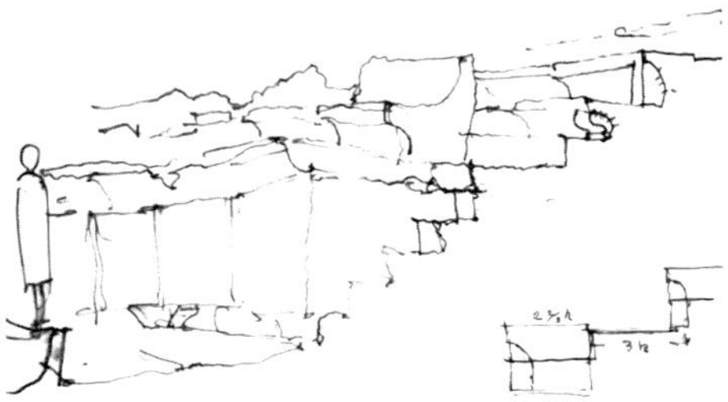

79. *Aalto's sketch of stone seats at the Theater of Dionysus in Athens (1953).*

Aalto's choices of itinerary to the sites of Delphi, Olympia, Mycenae, Epidaurus, and the Cycladic islands of Mykonos and/or Delos, could in the meantime suggest a storyteller's theme; a story with text and data fragments which could lead gradually to a partial restitution of actual events, until new evidence is uncovered to fill in the remaining black holes of Aalto's history.

One thing can be maintained, though. Alvar Aalto's destinations during this trip to Greece and the many sketches he was able to make while visiting ancient sites, required after all the flexibility, time and tranquility which a wanderer and lover of emblematic antiquities should enjoy. And, according to Elissa's words from Delphi, Alvar was able to take advantage of all three of these essential conditions, "a drawing pad under his arm to sketch Greek walls". It appears that the Aaltos spent at least two days in Delphi with an overnight stay at the Castalia Hotel.[100]

In spite of the demanding pressures raised by streaming projects at the Munkkiniemi office at the time, the Aaltos had seemingly decided to spend approximately 10 days in Greece, a rather long period compared to the previous shorter sojourns in Denmark, Switzerland and Italy. This was also perhaps necessitated in view of the expanded geographical distribution of places they visited and the more or less scanty transportation means available in the 1950s.

What then did Alvar Aalto seek during the trip to Greece in 1953, and what did he take with him back to Finland?

The sites Aalto visited during the second trip might in some way have added to a faculty of self-appraisal, particularly as it related to his early affinity towards the *classical* and its re-definition and role vis-à-vis the *modern*. Although most of the ideas and works during his *classical* beginnings were more or less romantic transliterations -if not imitations- of *Italian Renaissance* prototypes.[101]

A significant impulse from Aalto's intellect had to do with humanistic ideals, the physical expression of ancient Democracy, and the interplay of culture, nature and historicity. These important aspects he was most probably seeking to discern from his exposure to the complex monumental settings of the ancient sites. As the archaeologist Angeliki Kottaridi notes, [Classical] monuments represent "fingerprints of hand-made knowledge; they incorporate truth [*α-λήθεια*=that which can not be subject to oblivion

100. Reference from Elissa's handwritten letter from Delphi, op. cit.

101. The interest and affinity of architects towards Renaissance Italy has been amply documented. Already from the last quarter of the 19th century and the first decades of the 20th, architects and artists from the Nordic countries and Finland travelled extensively to Italy. In addition to the beauty and continuity in the history and the "culture" of aesthetics which Italian towns, city-states and their surroundings exemplify, this "one-way street" could be attributed to the neo-humanistic current prevalent in Europe during that period. Alvar Aalto was not an exception to this rule.
From another point of view, Italy's cultural continuity was not (violently) interrupted in the course of its history. This was not the case for either Finland or Greece, two "new" countries with a recent History of 100 and 200 years respectively, in spite of their cultural precedents and inheritance, and aside from their differences.

80. *Sketch by Aalto. Delphi from the top of the Theater with the columns of the Temple of Apollo, and in the background, the Tholos (1953).*

81. *Delphi from the top of the Theater (photo by K. Xanthopoulos. © KX Archive 2017).*

82. *Sketch by Aalto. Delphi from a lower level with the antiquities to the left of the ravine of Mount Parnassos where the springs of the Nymph Kastalia were located, and from where Pythia delivered her oracles (1953).*

83. *Sketch by Aalto of ruins and part of the Cyclopean retaining wall of the Temple of Apollo at Delphi. An example of Aalto's ability to enact along "aesthetic distance" (1953).*

84. *Cyclopean retaining wall near the Temple of Apollo at Delphi (photo by K. Xanthopoulos. © KX Archive 2017).*

85. *Aalto's sketch of ruins of Doric capitals and fragments lying on the ground at Olympia (1953).*

86. *Detailed sketch by Aalto of a marble block from a Temple at Olympia (1953).*

(Alvar Aalto sketches supplied by Timo Riekko © Alvar Aalto Archives, Jyväskylä).

=the non-oblivious]. The palimpsest body of Memory, apart from the expediencies of the times, is cohesive and indivisible. Vulnerable and highly fragile, it condenses the ethos of the past and belongs -as precious heritage- to the ones ever present."[102] There, he could have discovered the intricate forms adapted to geomorphic circumstances and dictates, with the *theater* being the focal point. He could have discerned the *heterotopia* of open-air "inner landscapes"[103] connecting and ordering asymmetries of and between physical parts, access paths and perspectives, all winding into an unconfined landscape. He could have further contemplated the ageing, the erosion and obsolescence of the monuments' ruins, at times possibly pairing his gaze with a melancholic mood, nurturing subtle nuances of imaginative constructs. After all, as Juhani Pallasmaa has aptly put it, it might have as well been that these "ruins and eroded settings", incomplete fragments of times past, were also stimulating Aalto's mind "to think of lives that have already disappeared, and to imagine the fate of their deceased occupants", as they carried such "a special evocative and emotional power".[104] Likewise, he could have been witnessing the way nature's micro-environment was blending with them in an ever changing amalgam signifying a perennial co-existence, in the course of the evolution of time.

Finally, he could have once again imagined the ideal measure –the Greek *μέτρον ἄριστον*– and the role exercised by the common citizen –the archaic "little man"– in his collective entourage, whether it be secular, political and/or religious.

During such discoveries, this time Aalto used his pencil instead of a camera, thus lifting the temporal image to a memorable embodiment which he could later recollect and transliterate into his own syntactic thesaurus. His perceptive gaze was not confined to a particular direction or distance. From the sketches he drew, it becomes obvious that its scope was panoptical, and where deemed necessary, also microscopic. He was therefore adapting his stance to a sort of *aesthetic distance*[105] to which the

---

102. Summary excerpt from a lecture given by Dr Angeliki Kottaridi on Dec. 13, 2018 at the Acropolis Museum of Athens, as part of a public discussion addressing to the general theme: *What do we ask from the ancient cultural heritage?* (*Τι ρωτάμε την αρχαία πολιτιστική κληρονομιά;*).

103. Ref. to "inner landscape" as an intermediary space with no observable form of its own. Göran Schildt, *Alvar Aalto and the classical tradition*. p. 132.

104. See Juhani Pallasmaa, "The mental power of fragments", in *Space, Place, Memory and Imagination...*, 2007, op. cit. p. 191.

105. The architect-philosopher/writer Panayotis Michelis had coined the term *aesthetic distance* to which he gave the following meaning: "As a dividing path, aesthetic distance is the way to oblivion from which a new world/cosmos is becoming visible as the old disappears. As a relational path, aesthetic distance is the way to memory, through which imagination has to pass, so as to catch and realize aesthetic ideas. Rightly so therefore the ancient Greeks were considering Mnemosyne the mother of Muses." He elaborates further that, "the favourable distance in space is of a material dimension and external, whereas the aesthetic is of a spiritual dimension distance and internal. With the former, vision and the eye perspective are being facilitated, whereas with the latter, it is the mind perspective which puts aside the insubstantial in order to give prominence to the essential... In architecture, which places its works in space, those of a bigger scale require from the onlooker a big distance, while those of a small scale a

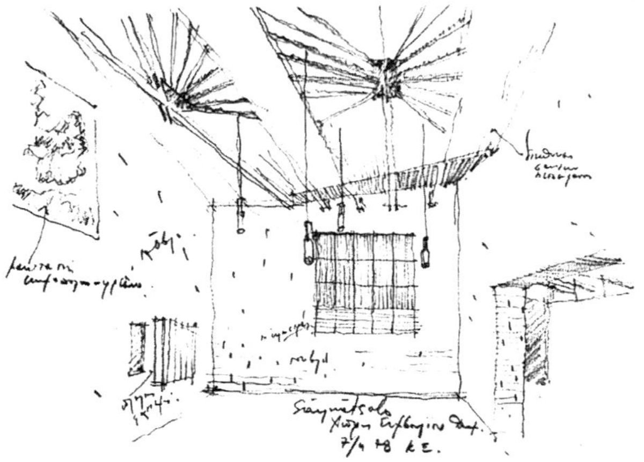

87. *Perhaps one of the most composite and inspirational achievement of Aalto's synthetic genius is the Säynätsalo complex (1949-1952). Conceived by the master-architect at a time of extreme intensity, Säynätsalo represents one of his peak achievements in which a number of analogies in terms of Greek classicism can be discerned. Aalto might have counterposed his distress after Aino's death with an energizing instinct for life's continuity and its creative thrusts, coupled with a sense of rejuvenation and a reinforced strength for self-determination, empowered by the presence of a young companion and colleague, his second wife Elissa.*
One year earlier, in 1948, Aalto and Aino had won the competition for the National Pensions Institute in Helsinki with their "Forum redivivum" entry. (project completed in 1956-1957), and, one year after Säynätsalo's completion, Aalto visited the classical sites of Greece. Both projects bear semiological meanings which could sustain valid narratives for Aalto's decisions to visit Greece in 1953.

88. *Perspective sketch of Säynätsalo's Council Chamber, crowning the outstandingly remarkable complex (photo and sketch K. Xanthopoulos. © KX Archive, 1978)*

general and the detailed were essentially expressed in their proper meaningful scale, both space- and time-wise.

No Aalto scholar made references to direct or obvious influences from his 1953 trip to Greece.

In 1955, however, Göran Schildt made allusion to a quote from Aalto, which connected the founding of the Museum of Finnish Architecture with an idea stemming from ancient Greek institutions. Accordingly, Aalto's vision was contemplating the Museum as "a forum in and through which Finnish architects could present constructive proposals". He used the term "cultural clearinghouse" in a sense reminiscent of Delphi, Delos and their "leagues" of cities, allied through political and cultural conventions.[106]

---

relatively smaller one, and each suggests a more favourable position than any other for its observation and study, as well as its comprehension [...] But the onlooker also needs to consider a favourable time distance with regard to architecture and its artefacts. [...] When imagination and memory are mobilized [...] we live in three time-present dimensions: the present of things that are present, the present of things that have preceded, and the present of those that will come in a future time. That is, each time that we observe present phenomena- things, we remember those that passed before and prognosticate those that are about to happen or to be. If memory nullifies distance of the past, imagination neutralizes the distance of the future. Both render the distance of the present its aesthetic meaning and dimension, when they capture he idea of a project, of the artefact. At the end, memory and imagination meet in the idea... As the most favourable place in space leads in a way to a pan-optical observation-survey, so is the most favourable point in time pan-mnemonic". In Panayotis Michelis, "Η αισθητική απόσταση και η γοητεία της σύγχρονης τέχνης/ Aesthetic distance and the charm of contemporary art", in *Αισθητικά Θεωρήματα/Aesthetic Theorems/* (1962 1st ed.). Vol. I, 3rd edition. P. and E. Michelis Foundation, Athens 1989, pp. 3-68. Also published in English in *Journal of Aesthetics and Art Criticism*, vol. XVIII, No. 1, Sept. 1959, pp. 1-45.

106. Göran Schildt, *Alvar Aalto; The mature Years*. Rizzoli, 1991, pp. 94-95.

Here too, additional metaphorical or pragmatic analogies could be attributed to Aalto's works, particularly to those integrating a number of civic and cultural functions, expressing the very idea and content of a city or of a community center.

It is in such projects where one could rather synoptically observe how the architect had organized and stratified the parts, fragments of integrated wholes; the *agoras* or *piazzas*, spaces for individual and collective activities; the interstices and the *heterotopic* conglomerate of independent elements; the blending and escalation of open spaces; the kinetic and processional scenarios; and in particular, the spaces for collective gatherings, democratic participation and governance. The latter are usually identified with either assembly rooms or lecture halls and theaters, as formal outbreaks culminating like little temples, amphitheaters, or "parthenons", peaking over all other physical parts in sensibly articulated complexes. Aalto could have also become increasingly aware of the ways time acted upon and modified man-made environments. Particularly during his "red brick" period, he seems to have consciously sought to make provision for some sort of built-in obsolescence, whereby his works would grow and age in harmony with nature and time. His flair for the organic form could have also stemmed from his earlier cultivated notion of the symbiosis between building, nature, and time. His intuition on this matter could have simply been upgraded by his 1953 phenomenological promenades around Greece's classical and other ancient sites.

Out of the sites Aalto had selected for his visits in 1953, perhaps the oddest was his hasty visit to the island of Mykonos. Most likely, he was already *au courant* of Le Corbusier's, Giedion's and Moholy-Nagy's appraisals with regard to the exceptional vernacular architecture of the Cyclades. He might have also been given advice from his new friend Schildt. Mykonos, carrying otherwise the charm of the dry, rough and "skeletal" qualities in this particular insular complex, could also reveal the white plasticity and irregular order, the organic growth and assemblages of houses, tightly intertwined along the network of its narrow and labyrinthine pathways, acting as air ducts. But here there was no "winding" sinuosity as produced by steep geological formations in graduating layers leading to a *Chora*, the top settlement –another *Acropolis*– as in many of other islands in the Aegean. There, contextualization and the integration of built forms into their entourage could exemplify a clearer and direct reference to a unique *paysagisme*; archetypes of *genius loci*. In this respect, Mykonos provided for a rather unassuming exemplar within the Cyclades, in spite of its coherently spellbinding nature.

Aalto had most likely very limited time while strolling around Mykonos' streets. His eye was seemingly caught by its emblematic windmills looming over the island's low hilltops, a subject which he had liked to sketch during his past trips to Spain (1951) and elsewhere. Aside from their eye-catching form and location, perhaps they were to him

89. *The 17th-century "Pentara" windmill of Mykonos appears in one of the two sketches by Aalto (photo from the 1970s).*

90. *Aalto's sketch of the "Pentara" windmill behind nearby houses in Mykonos (1953).*

91. *View of the "Paraportiani" church of Mykonos (photo by K. Xanthopoulos. © KX Archive, 1971).*

living proof of a centuries-old vernacular wisdom, testimonies to ingenious craftmanship, technology and function.[107]

Be that as it may, and given the protean nature of his intuitiveness, Aalto could not have missed standing for a while in front of the little white-washed church, the Paraportiani chapel of Mykonos, a paradigm of the anonymous ingenuity and skill of the island's local builders; not prone to swift sketching, to be forever admired as an image deeply locked into one's memory.

In spite of all this, there must have been another quite important reason explaining Aalto's decision to travel to Mykonos. It might have to do with the adjoining island of Delos, the locus of a confederation establishing the alliance of a number of ancient Greek cities. There is only one record that provides testimony to Aalto's probable visit to Delos. Ten years later, during a speech of his to SAFA architects, relating again to the significant cultural role of the Museum of Finnish Architecture, he noted:

> Those *of us* who have visited Delos, the main political and religious center of the Athenian Alliance, know that it did not directly serve this purpose -well that too, for it was the alliance's clearinghouse- but it served as exactly the kind of cooperative institution that I am talking of.[108]

---

107. From a notice sent by Mykonian writer and teacher Panagiotis Kousathanas (born 1945), it might be that Aalto had spent only few hours in Mykonos, having probably travelled from Piraeus aboard the *Semiramis*, which had just began to organize cruises to the Aegean islands (including Mykonos and Delos) as of 1953, with the co-operation of the Hellenic Tourist Organization-EOT.
It is through the same correspondence that Aalto's sketches were be identified with the "Pentara" windmill (see fig. 89), located next to and below the emblematic "Bonis" windmill complex (today a Farming Museum). The latter also appears in a second sketch drawn from a terrace just behind the triangular sails-fabric blades of the former. Aalto had apparently chosen the shortest pathway from the harbor, uphill to the above windmills ("Ano Myloi"), instead of the remotest group of the 5 windmills ("Kato Myloi") located close to the sea in the south-east. (Source: messages exchanged between Bjørn Røe, Panagiotis Kousathanas and the author, in August 20, 2018).
The Mykonos windmills were built from the 16th century onwards and played a very important role in the island's economic robustness, involved in the production and export of large quantities of hard-dried bread ("paximadia" in Greek).

108. See in Göran Schildt (ed.), *Alvar Aalto in His Own Words*, Otava Publishing Co, Helsinki 1997, p. 163.

EPILOGUE

A trip like this gives a boost to one's self-confidence.
(Alvar Aalto's letter to Aino from Greece in 1933)

As in his letter to Aino regarding his first experience in Greece, Aalto's second trip twenty years later must have increased his sense of "self-confidence" and his ability for spiritual contemplation.

He could however have had a third opportunity to make proof of his accumulated talent and intellectual maturity, when on April 23, 1963, Constantinos Doxiadis sent *Alvar Henrik Aalto* in his Tiilimäki address an "invitation of the Athens Technological Institute to participate in a conference of experts that will take place in Greece between July 6 and 13"[109] (see also p. 95). In his letter Doxiadis explained the purposes of the conference in view of the worsening condition of "human settlements". He also informed Aalto about some of the international personalities who would be attending, among others, Sigfried Giedion, Margaret Mead, Robert Matthew, Jean Gottmann and Pier Luigi Nervi. In addition, he mentioned that the meeting would "continue on board [a] ship in the Aegean Sea".

Ever since 1936, Doxiadis remained consistently faithful to the idea that there were important conceptual principles and elements, as well as methodological tools to be deducted from the study of classical Greek cities, that could be instrumental to contemporary urban design. His doctoral thesis *Raumordnung im griechischen Städtebau*

---

109. Letter copy supplied to the author by Timo Riekko / Alvar Aalto Archives, Jyväskylä.

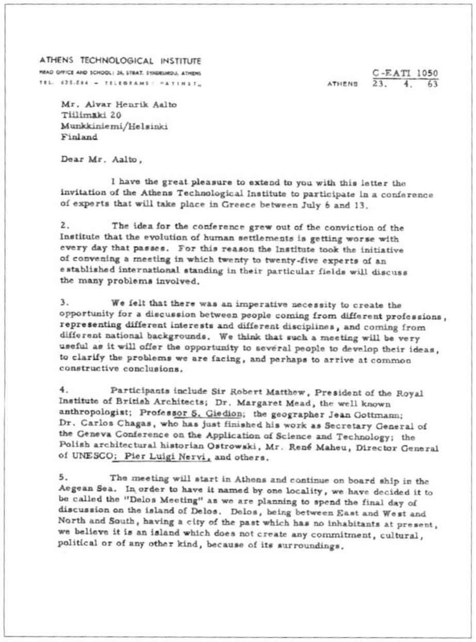

ATHENS TECHNOLOGICAL INSTITUTE
HEAD OFFICE AND SCHOOL: 24, STRAT. SYNDESMOU, ATHENS
TEL. 625.884 – TELEGRAMS: "ATINST"

C-EATI 1050
ATHENS 23. 4. 63

Mr. Alvar Henrik Aalto
Tiilimäki 20
Munkkiniemi/Helsinki
Finland

Dear Mr. Aalto,

I have the great pleasure to extend to you with this letter the invitation of the Athens Technological Institute to participate in a conference of experts that will take place in Greece between July 6 and 13.

2. The idea for the conference grew out of the conviction of the Institute that the evolution of human settlements is getting worse with every day that passes. For this reason the Institute took the initiative of convening a meeting in which twenty to twenty-five experts of an established international standing in their particular fields will discuss the many problems involved.

3. We felt that there was an imperative necessity to create the opportunity for a discussion between people coming from different professions, representing different interests and different disciplines, and coming from different national backgrounds. We think that such a meeting will be very useful as it will offer the opportunity to several people to develop their ideas, to clarify the problems we are facing, and perhaps to arrive at common constructive conclusions.

4. Participants include Sir Robert Matthew, President of the Royal Institute of British Architects; Dr. Margaret Mead, the well known anthropologist; Professor S. Giedion; the geographer Jean Gottmann; Dr. Carlos Chagas, who has just finished his work as Secretary General of the Geneva Conference on the Application of Science and Technology; the Polish architectural historian Ostrowski, Mr. René Maheu, Director General of UNESCO; Pier Luigi Nervi, and others.

5. The meeting will start in Athens and continue on board ship in the Aegean Sea. In order to have it named by one locality, we have decided it to be called the "Delos Meeting" as we are planning to spend the final day of discussion on the island of Delos. Delos, being between East and West and North and South, having a city of the past which has no inhabitants at present, we believe it is an island which does not create any commitment, cultural, political or of any other kind, because of its surroundings.

92. *Original letter by C. A. Doxiadis inviting Alvar Aalto to the Conference/Delos Symposium in Athens, between July 6 and 13, 1963 (C-EATI 1050/23.4.63). In it underlined by Aalto (?) are the names of S. Giedion and Pier Luigi Nervi! The second page states: "The Athens Technological Institute will be glad to cover all your expenses from the moment you arrive in Athens to the moment of your departure" (also underlined by Aalto). Before signing, Doxiadis concludes: "I am looking forward to receiving your answer as soon as possible". From evidence so far, Doxiadis never received an answer by Aalto (?) (copy of letter sent to author by Timo Riekko. © Alvar Aalto Archives, Jyväskylä).*
See full image on p. 95.

submitted at the Berlin Charlottenburg Technische Hochschule was only the proem for a series of inter-disciplinary research studies and conferences which culminated decades later with the so-called *Delos Symposia* (from 1963-1975).[110] In parallel, there was a considerable production of numerous papers and publications relevant to the issue, falling under the general term *Ekistics*, coined by Doxiadis himself.[111] The main issues brought forth had to do primarily with the structure and function, as well as with the concept of *human scale* related to the dimensions and size of cities, which could be accessible and experienced-felt throughout by their inhabitants; a challenge at stake most pointedly in modern cities. According to his positivist view, Doxiadis' rational analysis distinguished five basic categories of issues related to the study of human settlements, which were the object of his Ekistic's research orientations: Nature, Man, Society, Shells, and Networks. In fact, if taken as simple rubrics for the different aspects they could signify, the five categories of issues were also central to the Finnish master's pre-occupations, both in theory and indeed in his practice. The letter from Doxiadis to Aalto carried in this respect a certain justification.

Aalto would have undoubtedly been instrumental and active, had he chosen to participate. The fact that he decided not to do it, perhaps even omitting replying to

---

110. Constantinos Doxiadis' doctoral thesis on his analytical study and tracings of ancient Greek cities, which had been published in German as: *Raumordnung im griechischen Stadtebau* (Heidelberg: Kurt Vowinckel Verlag, 1937), had signified the start of a long research career by great architect and urban planner. His theory of *Ekistics*, and the subsequent *Delos Symposia*, were a natural follow-up to his initial theoretical preoccupations, as they were also partly reflected in his major urban projects around the world. The uninhabited island of Delos with its ancient ruins and theater was deliberately chosen for the summation and the final "declarations" of the Symposia for the quiet, serene and undistracted atmosphere it secured for the participating international erudites.
See: a) Dimitris Pikionis, "Η θεωρία του αρχιτέκτονος Κ.Α. Δοξιάδη για την διαμόρφωση του χώρου εις την αρχαία Αρχιτεκτονική"/"The theory of architect K.A. Doxiadis on the configuration of space in ancient Architecture", in *Dimitris Pikionis, Texts/Κείμενα*, op. cit., pp. 181-196. b) Constantinos Doxiadis' thesis translation by Panayiotis Tournikiotis: *Architectural Space in Ancient Greece*. Cambridge, Mass., MIT Press, 1972; c) Constantinos Doxiadis, *Ekistics: an Introduction to the Science of Human Settlements*, Oxford University Press, 1968; and d) Kostas Tsiambaos, *From Doxiadis' Theory to Pikionis' Work: Reflections of Antiquity in Modern Architecture*, Routledge, 2017.
Note: The author was privileged to have been invited to attend as a graduate student (Columbia University, N.Y.) the *Delos Symposium* of 1971. After returning to Greece, he worked as an architect-project manager at the Doxiadis & Associates main office in Athens from 1974-1976.

111. See i.e. Athens Center of Ekistics' study reports on ancient greek cities, such as: Arnold Toynbee, *An Ekistical Study of the Hellenic City-State* (1971), C.A. Doxiadis, *Η μέθοδος για την έρευνα των αρχαίων ελληνικών οικισμών/The Method for Research of Ancient Greek Settlements* (1972), and many others accessible from the C. A. Doxiadis Archives in Athens. Almost fifty years later, these studies have once again emerged at the forefront of today's research and indexing initiatives, also drawn upon the C.A.D., i.e. Martha Zarmakoupi, "Το ερευνητικό πρόγραμμα των αρχαίων ελληνικών πόλεων του Κ. Α. Δοξιάδη"/"The Research Program on the Ancient Greek Cities of C. A. Doxiadis", in *Ελληνική Αρχιτεκτονική στον 20ό ... /The Greek City in the 20th ...* op. cit., ed. Andreas Giacumacatos, 2016, pp. 314-324; and more recently, Kostas Tsiambaos, *From Doxiadis' Theory to Pikionis' Work...*, op. cit., 2017.

Doxiadis' invitation,[112] could not, however, be simply interpreted as paradoxical, ambiguous or idiosyncratic.

Doxiadis' modernity referring to antiquity and most particularly to the rational ideas set by Hippodamus of Miletus, had little to do with intuition, art, form and aesthetics.[113] His numerical and austere geometrical references did not quite correspond to Aalto's gaze and empathy for monuments and cities of past ages, and for what they could add to the intuitive deliberations in his mind. Or, had he considered that his trip to Greek sites ten years earlier had rather fully satisfied the scope of his interests about the nature of possible affinities between the *ancient* and the *modern*? A point which might suggest a plausible hypothesis.

So, Aalto did not respond to Doxiadis' invitation, as interesting, attractive, or redundant as he could have at first interpreted such opportunity. In addition, aside from facing anew a demanding and crucial phase of his extensive career, particularly in the 1960s, he had already satisfied to a great extent his will and ambitions with regard to large-scale city problematics, usually of abstract and theoretical nature. He might have even satisfied his earlier urge to be present amidst international celebrities and "expert" erudites. He had anyway rather aphoristic views on the platitude qualifying an "expert" or "expertise", as he had wittily expressed them in the past, with a pinch of sarcasm.

In sum, Doxiadis was and remained a visionary urban planner *par excellence*, utopian to a certain extent; Aalto, proportionately closer to both Pikionis and Despotopoulos, was and remained an architect *par excellence*. Scientific, multi-disciplinary and analytical or systems' approaches and theories were and could never have produced or identified his top works; Aalto's "classical" *pièces de résistance*.

Finally, all of the aforementioned theses and suppositions stand as fluttering issues to be further investigated, supplemented, and possibly to lead to more compliant narratives from future Aalto scholars.

The legacy of Aalto's works and spirit has proven to be *in aeternum* ardent "voyagers" in Greece, as has been and continues to be the case with many other countries.

In 1990, a significant volume of the architect's work was exhibited and celebrated at the Soutzos National Art Gallery in Athens following the accord and generous contribution of the Museum of Finnish Architecture. This event triggered the renewal of

93. *Constantinos A. Doxiadis at the Delos Theater during the closing session of the 1971 Symposium (photo K. Xanthopoulos. © KX Archive 1971).*

112. No copy of the same original letter was found in the C. A. Doxiadis Archives in Athens, as opposed to letters minutiously catalogued and kept in the case of other invitees.

113. For excellent documentation of Doxiadis' personality, ideas and theories, see: Dimitris Philippidis, *Κωνσταντίνος Α. Δοξιάδης (1913-1975)· Αναφορά στον Ιππόδαμο/Konstantinos A. Doxiadis (1913-1975); Reference to Hippodamus*, in particular Chapter B1, "Αριθμοί και γλώσσα/Numbers and language", Melissa Publishing House, 2015, pp. 67-88.

94, 95. *Front pages of the SADAS review (top) and the catalogue (bottom) of the Alvar Aalto Exhibition in Athens (1990).*

an essential dialogue between Greek and Finnish architects, and scholars on Aalto's legacy, which until then had remained relatively oblivious, or at best, incidental. In the Prologue of the exhibition catalogue, the members of the SADAS (the Greek SAFA) committee responsible for the Alvar Aalto exhibition had underlined the architect's role as "a link, a point of reference among other things, of the historical continuity and the qualitative consistency which distinguish in general the architectural creativeness in Finland", given "the importance of the architect's strong classical education on the development of his humanistic theory of the 'cosmos' and on his work as such".[114]

Also, already from the start of the present century, Aalto's sketches consecutively travelled at first to Athens (2000 and 2016), and afterwards to several other Greek cities as well. Sketches, photographs and related texts comprised the content linked to a second exhibition entitled *Finnish architects gazing upon Greece*.

Many examples could refer to Aalto's compositions of civic and cultural centers, often variably attributed to idealizations from his Mediterranean and Greek experience. Limited as the latter has been, his vision for such centers conveyed however symbolisms bringing them close to the philosophy of a *Delphic Center* adapted to modern times, as this has already been previously mentioned. Had he not after all expressed his wish for a revival of a socio-cultural *Amphictyonic League* ("league of neighbors"), adapted to the urban landscape of Finland and responding to contemporary social and cultural needs and accustomations of its citizens?

Didn't he in fact support an idea close to such ancient networking and participatory forms when he was envisioning the expanded role of the Museum of Finnish Architecture, or, for an equally important and multi-faceted role which his integrated city or community centers could fulfill?

But, as Shildt has again pointed out in reference to the Museum, the "proud House of Architecture in Helsinki, along with the dream of Finland as a cultural trend-setter, remained one of Aalto's many unfulfilled 'artistic fantasies'". Aalto had indeed imagined that "the cities and provinces of Finland could display their achievements there and vie for the best architectural ideas", following the examples of Delos and Delphi "with equally impressive (sic) results!"[115]

114. In preparation and during the time of the Alvar Aalto Exhibition in Athens, there was considerable participation and exchange of views on Aalto's legacy offered by a good number of architects and theoreticians from both Finland and Greece. Among them, Elissa Aalto, Aarno Ruusuvuori, Maija Kairamo, Juhani Pallasmaa, Martti I. Jaatinen, Asko Salokorpi and Kaisa Broner had responded to a series of questions addressed to them by Iossif Roilidis and Konstantinos (Kostas) Xanthopoulos, both now living in Finland. In addition several Greek architects had contributed with comments and articles referring to Aalto's oecumenical work and influence. See SADAS issue #1, period B, of December 1991, entitled *ΑΛΒΑΡ ΑΑΛΤΟ*.

115. Göran Schildt (ed.), *Alvar Aalto in His Own Words*, op. cit., pp. 94-95.

Furthermore, his early vision to transform by analogy Jyväskylä and the Finnish environment into some kind of idyllic northern "Tuscany" was also an unfulfilled "artistic fantasy". But it was a fantasy related more to "form" and "impression" than to "content" and "substance". "For me Italy represents a certain primitivism, characterized to an astonishing degree by attractive forms on a human scale", said he during an interview in 1954.[116]

In contrast Greece had reignited in Aalto's mature mind the value and importance of institutions, of the "content" more than the "form", with whatever remained from cities and sanctuaries in ruins. Their spatial order and disposition did not escape his attention and admiration either, as "forming a string of pearls."[117]

Later in 1972, during the age of philosophical contemplation, it was a Greek word which triggered Aalto's conscience, in the primal quest of re-interpreting architecture's purpose and content. In spite of his tremendous experience and acquired wisdom, he was inclined and had the power to ask once again: What is ***αρχιτεκτονική***? What does it essentially mean and convey?

> Like most Italian words, and most latin words before them, it [architettura] is a loan from Greek. And αρχιτεκτονική means something completely different than the art of building [rakennustaide]. It is related to the word archbishop -archtechnician, chief technician. But it does not mean that either. Because the situation at the time was that we were all architects. There was no difference between engineers and architects. But the word αρχιτεκτονική also included the idea of the humanist, and the whole mathematical aspect. It had a pretty broad range of meaning. The thing about Greek vocabulary was that nuances were so important; you could either use or not use a word.[118]

In 1976, Alvar Aalto ceased to be physically present.

96. *Alvar Aalto, Aino Marsio Aalto and Elissa Aalto grave in Hietaniemi Cemetery in Helsinki. Elissa Aalto's design included an original halved capital of Italianate Ionic order to suggesting here too a timeless allegory of the inextricable bonds relating the classical to the modern (photo by K. Xanthopoulos. © KX Archive, 2018).*

---

116. op. cit., Ref. to AA interview in *Casabella Continuità*, no 200, Feb./March 1954, p. 38.

117. op. cit., Ref. to AA speech to SAFA architects in 1963, SAFA Archives, in 1963. p. 163.

118. op. cit., Ref. to AA speech at the Helsinki University of Technology Centennial Celebration, Dec. 5, 1972. Aalto Archives. p. 282.

EPIMYTHIUM

Although Greece represented only a small fraction of Aalto's travelling choices, one could assume that his pursuits had evolved in a manner reminiscent of Constantine P. Cavafy's verses in his emblematic poem, *Ithaka*:

> Wise as you will have become, so full of experience, you'll have understood by then what these Ithakas mean.[119]

The Poet's symbolic verse proves to be true considering the interpretation of *classical spirit* brought to modern times, as demonstrated throughout in the architect's mature works, connecting art and architecture to man-society/culture-environment and nature.

---

119. Excerpt of verses from the Greek poet Constantine P. Cavafy's *Ithaka*, first published in the periodical *Γράμματα* [Letters] of Alexandria, in 1911. Translated into English by George Valassopoulo and published in T.S. Eliot's *The Criterion* with the support of E. M. Forster, in 1924. Also translated into Finnish by Aapo Junkola in 1984: "*Olet tullut viisaaksi, olet kokenut/ja silloin olet ymmärtänyt Ithakan merkityksen*".
Aside from the symbolism of the *Ithaka* verses which could attribute an "Odyssean" analogy to Aalto's extensive traveling and his related lifetime experiences, there is another interesting aspect which could express an affinity in the creative distinctiveness between Cavafy and Aalto.
As correctly noted by Dimitris Daskalopoulos and Maria Stasinopoulou at an interview (published in 18/8/2017 and reproduced-updated in Lifo magazine by Chr. Paridis in 13/8/2018), "*You can either imitate Cavafy in his own manner and therefore not be yourself, or pose as into a parody (parodize him). His poetic oeuvre could not develop into a School. And in spite of the fact that we* [Greeks] *have many other great poets, they belong to another era, mostly of the past. Cavafy is always modern. He does not belong to the past. He will always belong to the present.*"
And so it is with Alvar Aalto's architectural oeuvre.

Aalto's humanistic vision was as simple and clear as it was sophisticated, complex, and at times convoluted. Most probably all of the issues to which he addressed himself head-on will always provoke the intellect and raise hypotheses seeking new or complementary searches and interpretations, as time flows by.

It is not possible to imagine that Alvar Aalto's spirit and creativity, as repeatedly elevated and demonstrated through the totality of his work, will ever cease to be re-observed, re-interpreted and re-invented, *in aeternum*.

With his open, intuitive and unfathomed mind, he may always be read as an "open book" with a plethora of pages to supplement the real or fictive story of his traverse through life and architecture, through Greece and other places worldwide.

Et in Arcadia ego... [sum]

[next page] **97-100.** *Sketches and photos from Seinäjoki and Rovaniemi Centers, rendered and taken during the author's "Aalto pilgrimage" around Finland in March and April of 1978 (© K. Xanthopoulos/KX Archive).*

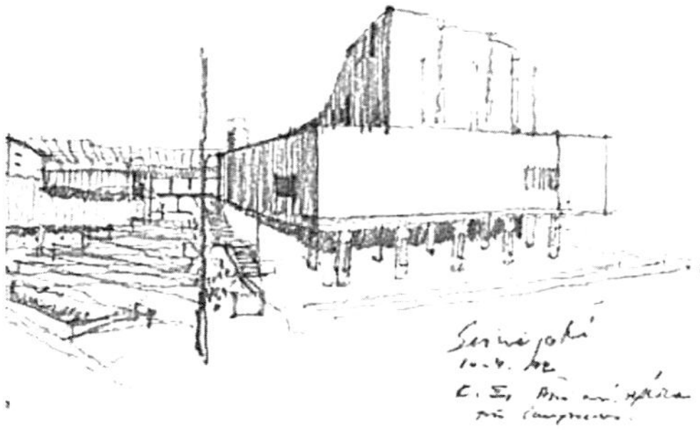

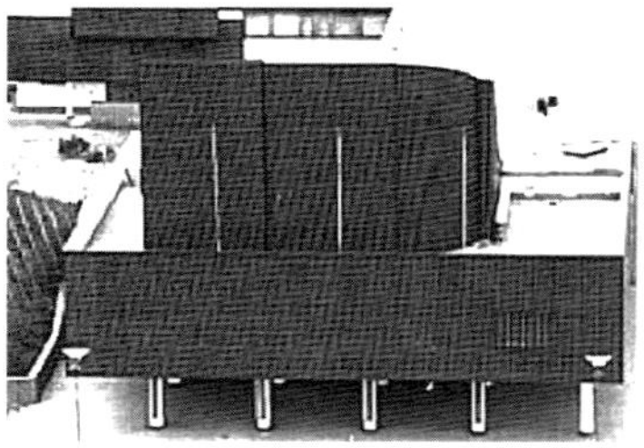

ACKNOWLEDGEMENTS

At first, my most sincere and deep gratitude is addressed to Professor emeritus Juhani Pallasmaa for having agreed to read my essay, offer his valuable comments and, not least, complement and enrich this work with a valuable introduction.
For a similar reason, my gratitude goes to Professor emeritus Dimitri Fatouros.
I also wish to thank Professor emeritus Tom Simons for initiating the idea to write about Aalto and Greece.

I owe special thanks to:

Professors of Architecture, Architectural Theory and History:
Dimitris Philippidis, Panayotis Tournikiotis (National Technical University, Athens), Andreas Giacumacatos (School of Fine Arts, Athens), Bjørn Røe (Trondheim-Norway), Marina Lathouri (London-England);

Architects:
Agni Pikioni and Dora Pikioni (Athens), Panayotis Tsakopoulos (Athens), Anthony Antoniades (Hydra-Greece), Agnes Couvelas (Athens), Tuula Pöyhiä (Jyväskylä and Helsinki) Architectural Historian Timo Tuomi (Helsinki);

Archivists:
Timo Riekko/Alvar Aalto Archives (Jyväskylä), Antti Aaltonen-Archive/Museum of Finnish Architecture (Drawings Collection, Helsinki), Anna Autio-Archive/Museum of Finnish Architecture (Image Requests, Helsinki), Ulf Johansson-Ludvika Municipality (Sweden), Marie Stahl/Archives, École Française d'Athènes, Ioanna Moraiti-Ghika Gallery/Benaki Museum, Giota Pavlidou/Constantinos A. Doxiadis Archives, Leti Krokou

Arvaniti/Ioannis Despotopoulos Archives/Archives of Modern Greek Architecture/Benaki Museum (Athens);
Librarian Maria Arvanitaki, ELIA-MIET, Hellenic Literary and Historical Archive (Athens);
Administrative Coordinator Caroline Dagbert, and Elspeth Cowell, Canadian Centre for Architecture, Montreal (Collection-Hazen Sise Fonds/Gift of Hazen Sise Family);
Senior Administrator Maria Martzoukou/The Finnish Institute (Athens);
Panagiotis Kousathanas (Mykonos-Greece, for his clarifications following Bjørn Røe's question on Alvar Aalto's trip on the island).

Finally, I am thankful to all those anonymous, willing and polite librarians and archivists from the following institutions, who facilitated my search and access to documents, books, and photographic collections, some of them rare and rather hard to discern:
Arkkitehtuurimuaseo Kirjasto-The Museum of Finnish Architecture Library, Helsinki
Helsingin yliopiston kirjasto (Kaisa Talo)-The Helsinki University Library, Helsinki
Kansalliskirjasto-The National Library of Finland, Helsinki
Museovirasto-The Finnish Heritage Agency Library and Archives, Helsinki
Αρχεία Νεοελληνικής Αρχιτεκτονικής/Μουσείο Μπενάκη-The Archives of Modern Greek Architecture/Benaki Museum, Athens
Πινακοθήκη Γκίκα/Μουσείο Μπενάκη- The Ghika Gallery/Benaki Museum, Athens
Les Archives de l'École Française d'Athènes
La Bibliothèque de l'Institut Français d'Athènes
Βιβλιοθήκη ΤΕΕ-The Technical Chamber of Greece Library, Athens

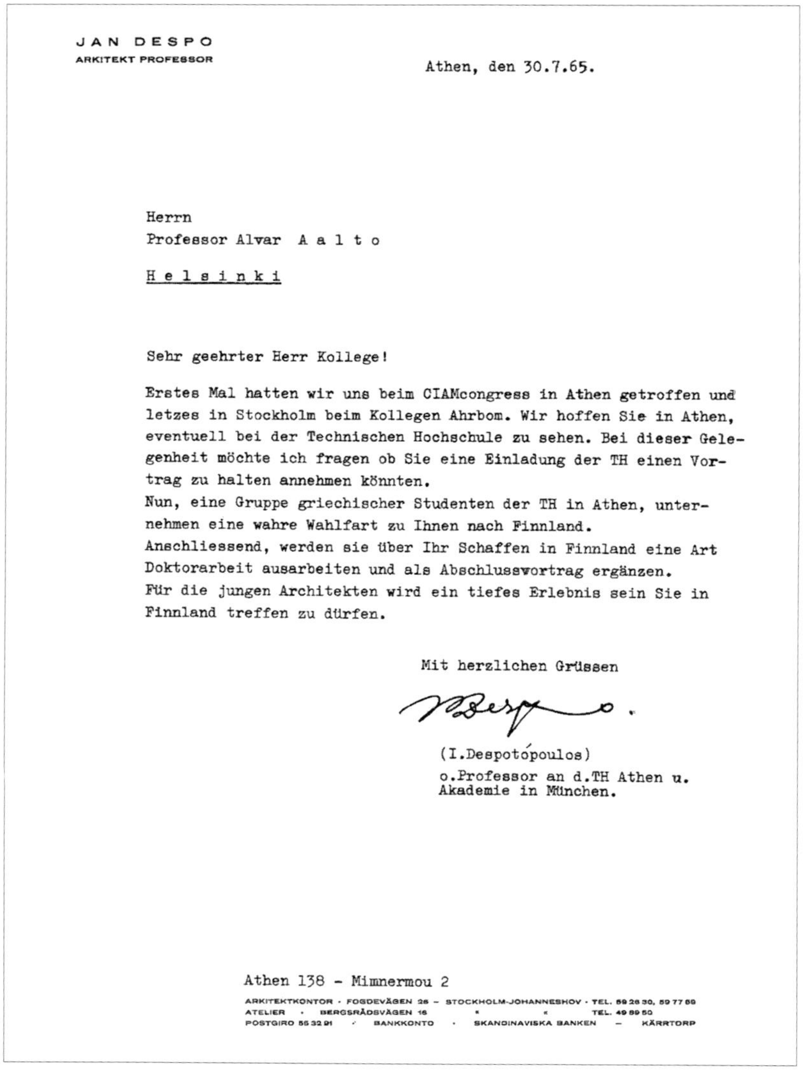

JAN DESPO
ARKITEKT PROFESSOR

Athen, den 30.7.65.

Herrn
Professor Alvar A a l t o

H e l s i n k i

Sehr geehrter Herr Kollege!

Erstes Mal hatten wir uns beim CIAMcongress in Athen getroffen und letzes in Stockholm beim Kollegen Ahrbom. Wir hoffen Sie in Athen, eventuell bei der Technischen Hochschule zu sehen. Bei dieser Gelegenheit möchte ich fragen ob Sie eine Einladung der TH einen Vortrag zu halten annehmen könnten.
Nun, eine Gruppe griechischer Studenten der TH in Athen, unternehmen eine wahre Wahlfart zu Ihnen nach Finnland.
Anschliessend, werden sie über Ihr Schaffen in Finnland eine Art Doktorarbeit ausarbeiten und als Abschlussvortrag ergänzen.
Für die jungen Architekten wird ein tiefes Erlebnis sein Sie in Finnland treffen zu dürfen.

Mit herzlichen Grüssen

(I.Despotópoulos)
o.Professor an d.TH Athen u.
Akademie in München.

Athen 138 - Mimnermou 2

ARKITEKTKONTOR · FOGDEVÄGEN 28 – STOCKHOLM-JOHANNESHOV · TEL. 59 26 30, 59 77 69
ATELIER · BERGSRÅDSVÄGEN 16 " " TEL. 49 89 50
POSTGIRO 55 32 91 · BANKKONTO · SKANDINAVISKA BANKEN – KÄRRTORP

ATHENS TECHNOLOGICAL INSTITUTE
HEAD OFFICE AND SCHOOL: 24, STRAT. SYNDESMOU, ATHENS
TEL. 625.584 – TELEGRAMS: "ATINST"

C-EATI 1050
ATHENS 23. 4. 63

Mr. Alvar Henrik Aalto
Tiilimäki 20
Munkkiniemi/Helsinki
Finland

Dear Mr. Aalto,

I have the great pleasure to extend to you with this letter the invitation of the Athens Technological Institute to participate in a conference of experts that will take place in Greece between July 6 and 13.

2. The idea for the conference grew out of the conviction of the Institute that the evolution of human settlements is getting worse with every day that passes. For this reason the Institute took the initiative of convening a meeting in which twenty to twenty-five experts of an established international standing in their particular fields will discuss the many problems involved.

3. We felt that there was an imperative necessity to create the opportunity for a discussion between people coming from different professions, representing different interests and different disciplines, and coming from different national backgrounds. We think that such a meeting will be very useful as it will offer the opportunity to several people to develop their ideas, to clarify the problems we are facing, and perhaps to arrive at common constructive conclusions.

4. Participants include Sir Robert Matthew, President of the Royal Institute of British Architects; Dr. Margaret Mead, the well known anthropologist; Professor S. Giedion; the geographer Jean Gottmann; Dr. Carlos Chagas, who has just finished his work as Secretary General of the Geneva Conference on the Application of Science and Technology; the Polish architectural historian Ostrowski, Mr. René Maheu, Director General of UNESCO; Pier Luigi Nervi, and others.

5. The meeting will start in Athens and continue on board ship in the Aegean Sea. In order to have it named by one locality, we have decided it to be called the "Delos Meeting" as we are planning to spend the final day of discussion on the island of Delos. Delos, being between East and West and North and South, having a city of the past which has no inhabitants at present, we believe it is an island which does not create any commitment, cultural, political or of any other kind, because of its surroundings.

ATHENS TECHNOLOGICAL INSTITUTE

C-EATI 1050
Page 2

6. The present letter is an invitation to you and one member of your family to attend this meeting. The Athens Technological Institute will be glad to cover all your expenses from the moment you arrive in Athens to the moment of your departure. This means transportation within Greece, accommodation, etc.

7. I very much hope that you will find it possible to fit this meeting in your schedule. I am sure that besides your valuable contribution to the conference, the meeting on board ship and visits to the islands of the Aegean will offer you an opportunity for relaxation. Enclosed is the programme of the meeting for your information.

8. I am looking forward to receiving your answer as soon as possible.

Yours sincerely,

C. A. Doxiadis

C. A. Doxiadis
President